AN EPIDEMIC OF EMPATHY IN HEALTHCARE

How to Deliver Compassionate, Connected Patient Care That Creates a Competitive Advantage

Thomas H. Lee, MD

Mc
Graw
Hill
Education

NEW YORK   CHICAGO   SAN FRANCISCO   ATHENS
LONDON   MADRID   MEXICO CITY   MILAN
NEW DELHI   SINGAPORE   SYDNEY   TORONTO

3 4 5 6 7 8 9 10   LCR   21 20 19 18 17

ISBN   978-1-259-58301-8
MHID   1-259-58301-5

e-ISBN   978-1-259-58631-6
e-MHID   1-259-58631-6

Library of Congress Cataloging-in-Publication Data
Lee, Thomas H., author.
  An epidemic of empathy in healthcare : how to deliver compassionate,
connected patient care that creates a competitive advantage / by Thomas H.
Lee.
      p. ; cm.
  Includes bibliographical references and index.
  ISBN 978-1-259-58301-8 (alk. paper) — ISBN 1-259-58301-5 (alk. paper)
  I. Title.
  [DNLM: 1. Delivery of Health Care—organization & administration.
2. Empathy. 3. Attitude of Health Personnel. 4. Delivery of Health
Care—economics. 5. Patient-Centered Care—organization & administration.
W 84.1]
  RA971
  362.1068—dc23
                                                              2015033589

McGraw-Hill Education books are available at special quantity discounts
to use as premiums and sales promotions or for use in corporate training
programs. To contact a representative, please visit the Contact Us pages at
www.mhprofessional.com.

For Soheyla

Contents

Acknowledgments

IF AN EPIDEMIC of empathy is an idea whose time has come, it is because of the timeliness of the convergence of a series of ideas from various key colleagues. I hope this acknowledgment of their deep influence on this book will also serve as an abbreviated syllabus for readers who might want to go more deeply into some of the themes I have woven together. Individually and collectively, the work of these colleagues provides important insights into healthcare's current state and where healthcare should go.

For insight into the nature of strategy in a competitive healthcare marketplace, there is no better place to begin than with the work of Michael E. Porter, my colleague, coauthor, and friend from Harvard Business School. Over the last few decades, Michael has defined the meaning of strategy for business in general. His work on healthcare has helped clarify why an overarching strategic goal is important for every organization and why that goal should be to create value for patients, determine what multidisciplinary teams should look like, and decide what kind of information and incentives those teams need to drive improvement.

For insight into the nature of the overall healthcare marketplace and the dynamics related to real competition (as well as efforts to frustrate competition), I turn to Leemore Dafny, a Kellogg School economist who is perhaps best known for her work on payer and provider consolidation, illustrating how it leads to weaker competition and higher prices. Like many clinicians, I have long been leery of thinking about healthcare as a marketplace, anticipating potentially perverse consequences if patients have to act like consumers and try to make trade-offs between quality and price. But no model of paying for healthcare is perfect, and all those models can have a range of adverse effects. Dafny and some of her economics colleagues inspire confidence that competition in a value-driven market has great potential to drive improvements in quality and efficiency, especially if providers embrace competition and learn to trust market forces. All stakeholders, including providers, will trust market forces more if providers are actively engaged market participants by, for example, being transparent with their quality data. Porter's and Dafny's work tell us what we have to do and why we have to do it.

But how to get that work done? University of Chicago sociologist Ronald Burt's book on social capital *Brokerage and Closure: An Introduction to Social Capital* is one that I have given to virtually every colleague working directly with me in managing healthcare delivery. It provides a clear and useful structure for learning (increasing variation in what is done by brokering ideas) and then converging on best practices (closure). Social capital is at least as important as financial capital to the ability of healthcare providers to compete in the era ahead, and corporate boards should give it the lion's share of their attention.

No one's name appears more often in this book than that of Nicholas Christakis, the Yale social network scientist whom I met when he was launching his extraordinary work at Harvard. From Nicholas, I have learned how epidemics of values and emotions can spread from person to person to person and how to think of a group of people as an organism. If the work of Porter, Dafny, and

Burt defines the big picture, Christakis characterizes the nature of the work to be done closer to the ground.

Then there is the work that is not included in this book and is conspicuous by its absence. By that, I mean the nuts-and-bolts details of the kinds of programs and actions that can improve patients' experiences. For those details, I refer readers to the work of my colleague Jim Merlino, former chief experience officer of Cleveland Clinic and author of the widely praised bestselling book *Service Fanatics: How to Build Superior Patient Experience the Cleveland Clinic Way.*

I also have been deeply influenced by my colleagues at Press Ganey, most notably Deirdre Mylod, who was the first and the most persistent in saying that the reduction of suffering should be the performance goal to be measured and managed, and Christy Dempsey, our chief nursing officer, who defined compassionate connected care as the way to reduce suffering. Pat Ryan became the CEO of the company in 2012 and made these goals the focus of Press Ganey even before talking to me about joining.

I allude throughout the book to the work and wisdom of many colleagues on the provider side. (I won't single out any to minimize the risk of slighting others.) I do, however, want to thank Beverly Merz and Gregg Dipietro for their help in preparing this manuscript and Casey Ebro at McGraw-Hill for having the confidence that we could produce the book in a rather short time frame and the great editing and interpersonal skills that made that happen.

Finally, the very idea of this book was that of my wife, Soheyla Gharib, MD. She suggested it one day over breakfast and did not complain when weekends and evenings were then lost to it. She's a wonderful physician, and I often think of how I would not want to do anything in my medical practice that would disappoint her.

She provides the norm. In this and many other ways, the influence of our relationship on my work is a demonstration of Nicholas Christakis's ideas about social networks in action.

Introduction

In early 2014, my colleagues and I started publicly asking the question "Can we create an epidemic of empathy in healthcare?" We sometimes received puzzled looks in return. The Ebola epidemic was just getting under way, after all, and the word *epidemic* evoked panic, not comfort. Empathy was something that was respected and sought by everyone in healthcare, of course—especially patients—but most clinicians viewed empathy as a personal characteristic; either you had it or you didn't.

Nevertheless, within seconds of hearing the phrase "epidemic of empathy," most people smile, nod, and understand, and many say that it is an idea whose time has come. An epidemic is an outbreak that pushes the prevalence of a condition to higher than normal levels; that push comes through contagion: transmission from person to person to person. In the classic use of the term, *epidemic* refers to the spread of infectious diseases. But other medical problems (e.g., diseases caused by cigarette smoking) also rise and decline in the same pattern as Ebola and other infections.

The idea that values might spread in the same patterns as infectious diseases and that empathy might actually be contagious can be traced to the work of the social network scientist Nicholas Christakis. In a startling 2007 paper in the *New England Journal of Medicine*, he and his colleagues showed that obesity appears to spread through social ties.[1] They demonstrated that if a friend of a friend of yours gains weight, you are more likely to gain weight even if you do not know that friend of a friend. A year later, they showed the same patterns with cigarette smoking and smoking cessation.[2]

Christakis and his colleagues subsequently went on to show that emotions such as happiness and social values such as generosity to charities also spread with similar patterns within social networks. In short, social norms are influencing our behaviors all the time, often too subtly for us to notice. If being overweight seems socially acceptable, having those supersized French fries may seem a reasonable choice. If others around us are picking up their litter, we do, too.

In healthcare, unfortunately, nonempathic care had become epidemic during the period leading up to this research by Christakis (who is, incidentally, a palliative care physician by training). The problem is not that medical schools can no longer find good human beings to train as physicians or that money has perverted the profession. The problem is progress itself.

Over the last century, particularly the last 50 years, research has yielded marvelous advances. But one of the side effects has been that clinicians have increasingly narrow fields of expertise and that it takes more and more of them to deliver state-of-the-art care. The joke in medicine is that doctors today have a choice of learning more and more about less and less until they know everything about nothing—or they can know less and less about more and more until they know nothing about everything.

Where there is humor, look for truth (a recommendation that comes from both George Bernard Shaw and Sigmund Freud). Neither option feels very good, but most young physicians choose the former, focusing on narrow issues so that they can master all the science even if it means eschewing the broader challenge of taking care of the person in whom the medical issues are playing out. Even within specialties, real expertise means becoming a sub-specialist or a sub-subspecialist. At major cancer centers, for example, physicians tend to focus on one cancer and one cancer only: the lymphoma doctors do not see multiple myeloma patients, and the myeloma doctors do not see lymphoma patients.

I have nothing against this trend toward sub-subspecialization. In fact, I routinely seek out such experts for my own patients and friends. In the vast majority of cases, seeing such an expert doesn't make a difference in patient survival or in the degree of patient disability. However, every now and then it does make a difference. When physicians are seeing patients with a specific disease all day, every day, they gain experience, and with that experience comes the ability to sense deviations from the norm. Sometimes that experience enables them to decide that a patient's course is not as it should be and that his or her symptoms warrant closer scrutiny. At other times, that experience enables them to live with uncertainty.

For example, a woman I know was evaluated for hip pain, and the x-rays showed an unusual abnormality of her bones. Her x-rays didn't fit any pattern that her physicians could recognize, and she was scheduled for surgery to remove the abnormal bone. The night before her operation, she was visited by a very experienced orthopedist who was a friend, not her actual doctor. She asked the orthopedist if she was doing the right thing by having the operation. He hesitated, not wanting to disrupt her care and play doctor when he was there only as her friend. But then he said, "I don't think I would do it."

"Why not?" she said. "Do you know what I have?"

"No," he answered. "But I have seen almost everything bad there is related to hips, and this doesn't look like any of the bad things I have seen."

She decided that if he wasn't unnerved by what he saw on the x-ray, she could cancel her surgery and pursue a watch-and-wait strategy. It's been 25 years since she made that decision. Her diagnosis is still a mystery. And she is still watching and waiting.

At its best, the trend toward sub-subspecialization allows patients to see teams of clinicians (not just doctors alone) who are deeply experienced in meeting the needs of patients with a specific medical condition. One of my favorite examples is Mayo Clinic's approach to breast cancer. Each patient has her own team assembled in accordance with her unique needs. It may include, in addition to oncology subspecialists, a primary care physician, a nutritionist, a physical therapist, and even a family therapist. Mayo Clinic knows that the patients who go there for breast cancer have needs beyond the treatment of their malignancy. They have other health issues, they have fears and anxiety, and they have worried families. The best teams in healthcare are organized holistically to meet most or all of the needs of patients with a specific condition, not just to help a sub-subspecialist do what he or she does best.

But it doesn't always work this way. In most of medicine, the trend toward specialization has come at the expense of that holistic approach to the patient. Because of medical progress and the resulting complexity of diagnosis and treatment, the role models in medicine have shifted from the compassionate generalist physicians—the Marcus Welbys—to the superspecialized experts who understand the most intricate mechanisms of disease and every now and then use those insights to pull off an amazing save. Bearing witness to a patient's suffering is no longer the definition of a great physician; saving a patient who would otherwise have died has become the goal. Younger physicians have adopted as their role models the superspecialists who are going for the saves.

Patients love stories about great saves, and so do hospital marketing teams and development officers. The problem is that healthcare cannot be only about going for great saves. Meeting patients' needs well and reliably is going to require a new orientation for clinicians, and that new orientation is going to require great teamwork, including new ways of working with colleagues and new ways of relating to patients.

It's also going to require clarity on the real goals of healthcare. As providers have felt the financial pressure to become more efficient, questions have naturally arisen: Efficient at what? What are we trying to achieve through healthcare? These questions have become increasingly pressing because if you do not have clarity on what you are trying to achieve, the pursuit of efficiency feels like a mildly perverse game in which you are trying to see what you can cut without creating too much of a ruckus.

Healthcare reform came to Massachusetts a little earlier than it did to the rest of the country, and as it progressed, my colleagues at Partners HealthCare System started stewing about the ultimate goal of healthcare. We knew we were not in the immortality business, and we also knew that we could not restore many patients to full health. One of my colleagues, Cindy Bero, an information technology expert who had two parents with serious neurological diseases, captured the challenge best. She said, "We're all going to die, and most of us are going to go downhill before we die. But we all want peace of mind that things are as good as they can be, given the cards that we have been dealt."

At the time, I joked that she had come up with a great slogan for our organization: "Peace of mind as you go downhill and die." The others in the room laughed, but before the laughter died down, someone said what many were thinking: "That *is* what we are supposed to do. Give people peace of mind that things are as good as they can be, given the cards that they have been dealt."

That insight raised a series of troubling questions: If peace of mind is what we are supposed to produce, how well do we do it? Are we organized around that goal? Do we do things that systematically erode it?

I understood that in my best moments as a doctor I took the time to look patients in the eye, recognize what worried them, and work to allay their fears Part of that work was to do what my medical training prepared me to do: enable them to live as long as possible and to be as functional as possible along the way.

But another part of that work was what is now called emotional labor: make the effort to see things from their perspectives, understand their fears, and convey that to them. Beyond that, providers need to assure patients that they are going to work with all their colleagues to ensure that, well, things are as good as they can be, given the cards the patient has been dealt.

That emotional labor is the core of empathy. Pretty much everyone—although not quite everyone—in healthcare knows how to do it. In fact, I think most clinicians enjoy it; otherwise, they probably would have sought another, less complicated type of work. But turning on empathy for the patients one likes or identifies with is not enough. Empathic care should be the norm, not the exception. Also, some physicians, nurses, physical therapists, and other personnel are better and more reliable in delivering empathic care than others.

Can we use the insights from social network science to spread the values of these caregivers? Can we use our growing ability to capture and analyze data on what patients are going through to identify opportunities for improvement and then drive actual improvement? Can we help healthcare personnel be the way they want to think of themselves and be that way all the time?

I think the answers to these intertwined questions are all yes. The reason I wrote this book is not to give a pep talk to my colleagues. I wrote it because I believe that healthcare is at a special moment. We now have clarity on what we need to improve and why we need to improve it. The science and technology of measuring whether we are meeting patients' emotional and physical needs has advanced tremendously. We are ready to apply insights into social capital, social networks, and the use of financial and other incentives to drive a real epidemic of empathy.

What would an epidemic of empathy look like? There would be a steady, relentless increase in the percentage of clinicians and other personnel who are clearly tuned in to what is really happening to patients and their families. Coordinated and empathic care would not seem to patients as miraculous and unpredictable as a lightning bolt of love (*un colpo di fulmine*, as the Italians put it). Instead, delivery of such care would become the norm; it would become increasingly fundamental to the way healthcare personnel saw themselves.

What would it take to get there? One critical step is to create the shared vision of what empathy means; that work has been in progress for several years and is accelerating. Organizations such as the Schwartz Center for Compassionate Healthcare and the Arnold P. Gold Foundation have been exploring and promoting the concept of compassionate care. The Cleveland Clinic empathy video,[3] which has been viewed by millions around the world, is just one example of how healthcare organizations are finding new ways to remind their personnel of what their patients are going through.

To get there, we also need a new language that compels a response. Use of the word *suffering* by clinicians and leading medical journals was rare in the past because the term was considered overly emotional. In fact, I published an article in the *New England Journal of Medicine* about that term that was titled "The Word That Shall Not Be Spoken" in November 2013.[4] But on February 18, 2015, just 16 months later, the *New York Times* ran a major story by Gina Kolata on its front page about how the reduction of suffering had become the overarching goal for many healthcare organizations around the country.[5] Now, the word *suffering* is being invoked with increasing frequency by healthcare providers with the goal of reminding clinicians of the anxiety, confusion, and uncertainty that their patients endure.

There are other words that rarely came up in healthcare management discussions in the past that I am sure will become explicit foci in the years ahead, such as *fear, trust, hope, peace of mind, exhaus-*

tion, helplessness, and *loneliness.* These emotions matter to patients, but they are also of great relevance to clinicians and the rest of the healthcare workforce. Organizations that can address such issues effectively will have a competitive business advantage, along with pride in what they are doing.

A third critical step is to understand what drives patients' suffering. The pain and disability that result from their diseases are major factors, of course, but so is the avoidable suffering that results from the dysfunction of the delivery system: the delays, the uncertainty about what is going to happen next, the chaos that results when clinicians are not coordinating their efforts closely. Issues such as convenience, food, and parking are trivial to patients compared with these concerns.

A fourth step is to collect enough data so that meaningful analyses can be directed at potential units of improvement, including the individual physician. Patients are the only ones who can comment on whether they have peace of mind and whether their needs are being met. Ideally, these data would be akin to a vital sign (e.g., heart rate, blood pressure, and body temperature): information collected on every patient at every encounter. Approaching that ambitious goal means using electronic surveying technologies, collecting e-mail addresses on every possible patient, and sending surveys to seek information after every hospitalization or office visit.

To date, healthcare organizations have used carpet-bombing strategies, in which all personnel are urged to be more empathetic. With increasing ability to profile the performance of individual physicians, many organizations have been using the bad apple approach, focusing on encouraging improvement among the physicians who seem to be doing the worst. But to create an epidemic of empathy, organizations need to use other approaches as well. They need to find the personnel who are most reliable in their delivery of empathic care and enlist them in spreading whatever it is that they are doing right. They need to assemble a critical mass of empathic clinicians so that they are harder to ignore as anomalies. Another important tactic is to find the personnel who are most isolated from the organization's culture and bring them in.

The goal is to make well-respected, connected personnel who understand empathic care become the drivers of its spread—in effect, the Typhoid Marys of the empathy epidemic. The adoption of their practices can be accelerated by the use of financial and nonfinancial incentive systems that remind clinicians that every patient encounter is a high-stakes event not just for the patient but for the clinician as well. The University of Utah's pioneering work in transparency—putting all patient comments about every physician online on its find-a-doctor website—has brilliantly shown the powerful effects of the knowledge that every patient has a chance to offer a comment online. As one orthopedist put it, it forces him to be at the top of his game for every single patient.

This work is noble and consistent with the best professional values of medicine, but it's also good business strategy. We are entering a new healthcare marketplace in which providers are going to be competing on the right things: meeting patients' needs and doing so as efficiently as possible. That competition makes providers uncomfortable, but it is the best possible business context for driving progress toward a better and more affordable healthcare system. The providers that recognize that competition and plunge in are most likely to succeed and even thrive. As for the providers that do not embrace the competition, well, their prognosis is worrisome at best.

Part of embracing healthcare's competitive new environment should be creating an epidemic of empathy within healthcare organizations. Despite the added pressure, I haven't met a clinician yet who thinks there is anything wrong with that. In fact, everyone in healthcare knows that we have a problem and that even patients whose care is technically excellent often do not feel cared for. The cure for this disease is to create an epidemic of our own, and I think we know how.

1 | The Problem

THE IRONY IS difficult to ignore. We are living in a golden age of medicine, but it doesn't feel that way.

Over the last half century, medical progress has taken diseases that were the equivalent of death sentences and turned them into chronic conditions that are treatable and sometimes curable. The mortality rate from heart attacks has fallen from 40 percent to about 5 percent. Lymphomas and other cancers, along with infections such as hepatitis C and HIV, can be controlled or eradicated with medications. Tests for genetic markers in cancers are identifying treatment options that are giving hope and sometimes extending life for patients with advanced disease.

Patients are thrilled by the potential of modern medicine to help them lead longer and healthier lives, but they worry that the benefits will be beyond their reach, that they will not be able to afford insurance that gives them access to excellent doctors and hospitals or these marvelous advances. They are anxious about whether their clinicians are actually talking to one another and coordinating their efforts and whether errors will result. They worry that no one is paying attention to the big picture of their personal goals and needs.

These concerns are not the neuroses of a few malcontents. In a national survey of 800 recently hospitalized patients, more than 80 percent said that compassionate care is very important to successful medical treatment, but only 53 percent felt that the current healthcare system provides it.[1] In this survey, fewer than 70 percent of patients gave their physicians high ratings (9 or 10 on a 10-point scale) on elements of compassionate care (Table 1.1). If their physicians had received similar grades in the courses required for them to reach medical school, they wouldn't be doctors.

Table 1.1 Percentage of Patients Rating Their Physicians' Demonstration of Compassionate Care Elements Highly

Element of Compassionate Care	Patients Rating Physician's Demonstration of the Element Highly, %
Show respect for you, your family, and those important to you	68
Treat you as a person, not just a disease	66
Listen attentively to you	59
Express sensitivity, caring, and compassion for your situation	58
Consider the effect of your illness on you, your family, and the people most important to you	51
Strive to understand your emotional needs	49

Data excerpted from Beth A. Lown, Julie Rosen, and John Martilla, "An Agenda for Improving Compassionate Care: A Survey Shows About Half of Patients Say Such Care Is Missing," *Health Affairs* 30, September 2011: 1772–1778.

As disappointing as modern medicine may be for patients, the harsh reality is that it doesn't feel so great for doctors, either, or for other clinicians delivering patient care. There is so much that can and should be done for patients today, the work of being a doctor or nurse often feels like an endless checklist. On the one hand, advanced electronic medical records can put everything that is happening to a physician's patients in front of that physician. On the other hand, the amount of activity and knowledge that a physician ought to know can be overwhelming. When I click on the "in basket" in my electronic medical record system, I feel like a fire hose has been turned on and is blasting me against the wall.

It is, of course, a good thing that we clinicians have access to comprehensive information on our patients and reminders of all the things we need to do. We are doing a better job as a result. The irony is that we *felt* like we were doing a better job back when there was less to know and less we could do.

For example, just a few years ago, when there were no treatments for hepatitis, all clinicians could do was make the diagnosis and say something about the prognosis. Today there are complicated (and expensive) drug regimens to discuss and choices to be made, and most clinicians do not feel comfortable leading those conversations.

In that simpler time, a doctor would walk into a patient's room, and the patient and family would snap to attention, hanging on the doctor's every word. Back then, the respect for doctors and other clinicians throughout society was palpable. It certainly still exists today, but what is also palpable and often more powerful than respect among patients is the fear that clinicians do not have their act together. There are so many clinicians involved in giving sophisticated care that patients get conflicting and confusing messages all the time and cannot help wondering if their clinicians are talking to one another or listening to patients.

What Happened?

How did we get to a point at which empathy—or the lack thereof—could be a problem in medicine? When so many doctors, nurses, and other personnel are working so hard in the care of patients, why do patients worry that no one is paying attention to them and their real concerns? When so many resources are being invested in it, who is to blame for the confusion that so often characterizes modern healthcare?

If these problems had simple explanations, they might have simple solutions. If the people working in healthcare were incompetent, they could learn new skills. If their characters were flawed, admission criteria and hiring practices could be tightened. If financial incentives were rewarding the wrong behaviors, those incentives could be changed. But the fact is that our difficulties in delivering compassionate and coordinated care are not the result of bad guys who can be rounded up, retrained, or eliminated.

The root cause of our problems is medical progress itself. With progress has come an increase in the number of clinicians required to deliver state-of-the-science medical care. How many different hospital personnel do patients having routine cardiac or orthopedic surgery come in contact with? It varies among institutions, but when anyone bothers to count, the figure is often 100 or more.

These clinicians have narrower and narrower expertise and are focused on specific organs and diseases, often overlooking the issues of the patient as a whole. I got my first glimpse of this dynamic in the late 1980s. Pacemakers were just at the point of becoming small computers, able to do much more than nudge the heart electrically if it stopped beating for more than one second. The newer pacemakers could crank up the heart rate if the body needed more blood flow, such as when a patient was running up the stairs.

As pacemakers became more complicated, a new subset of cardiologists emerged: pacemaker experts. I sent one of my primary care patients to our pacemaker expert, who implanted the device and saw her in the office every few months afterward to be sure it was operating correctly. The pacemaker worked flawlessly. The problem was that my patient liked the pacemaker expert too much.

They were immigrants from the same country, and when they saw each other, they could speak their native tongue and talk about restaurants in the old country and where to get their favorite foods in their new one. The pacemaker expert was warm and personable and enjoyed the conversations until he realized that my patient was calling him about issues that really should have been my focus as her primary care physician. She would call him (instead of me) about headaches and urinary tract infections and nagging colds and coughs.

At first, he would do his best to address those issues, but then he tried to explain to her how the system was supposed to work. It was a little confusing because I am both a cardiologist and a primary care physician, and so she assumed that he was, too. Finally, he put it very bluntly to her: "Lady, I only take care of the machine."

At that point she got it. But she didn't feel good about it.

At least my pacemaker expert and I knew each other, saw each other in the hallways, and wanted to work as a team. All too often, the "team" of clinicians who contribute to the care of patients is loosely organized and the team members have poor communication with one another. Frequently, they have not even met before and would not recognize each other if they passed in the hall. They are working hard but often are not working together.

With so many clinicians involved in the care of patients, being a primary care physician feels more like being an air traffic controller than like being a heroic healer. Time to listen to patients, to bond with them, to experience the deep appreciation of a family after enduring a difficult passage together seems like a quaint notion from another era.

To make matters worse, medicine has become a lonelier endeavor. When there was less to do, there was more time to sit and talk both with patients and with one's colleagues. Don't get me wrong; we were plenty busy in the old days and can all remember all-nighters of frantic activity until dawn and reinforcements arrived. But we were more likely to be working in groups, and there was time and opportunity for conversations about scientific advances relevant to our patients, for gossip relevant to our social lives, and for professional and personal norms to develop. Today hospitals feel more like airports, with everyone hurrying from one place to another with little time for informal interactions about patients and casual talk about the rest of life.

In short, medicine has become a busier but simultaneously more isolated life for the people who deliver medical care. Outpatient physicians often do not go to the hospital anymore, because hospitalists take charge of care once patients need to be admitted. Hospitalists do not venture outside of hospitals, and so they do not see patients after discharge or the other clinicians who assume their care. No one goes down to the basement to see the radiologists because the reports and images are available on the computer, and so the radiologists feel that their job is interpreting images rather than being part of a team taking care of patients.

In this isolation and amid such frenzied activity, empathy for patients is supposed to be everyone's job, but that often means it is no one's job. That makes it unlikely for empathic care to become a social norm that spreads from clinician to clinician to clinician.

Healthcare in Chaos

The chaos that characterizes modern care was underscored for me when one of my primary care patients developed a mysterious and painful rash on his legs. He was in his late seventies and had a long list of medical problems that had been held in check for a long time, though but just barely. He had coronary artery disease and had had bypass surgery. He had a history of prostate cancer that had spread to his bones, but the cancer had been slowed to a standstill by the injection of medications every three months. He had several less threatening medical conditions, each of which was annoying but not much more. He was a tough guy—a former marine—and whatever problems he had, he was ready to tolerate them with minimal or no complaints.

But one day he woke up with swollen joints and a painful rash on his legs, and he could barely get out of bed. His rash and his joint problems did not fit neatly into any of the common problems I saw in my medical practice, and he did not respond to anti-inflammatory agents such as ibuprofen or even narcotic-strength painkillers. We admitted him to Brigham and Women's Hospital, the teaching hospital where I work, and he was seen by teams of experts in dermatology, infectious disease, oncology, cardiology, and rheumatology, among others.

At hospitals like mine, we usually need only a day or so to pin down the cause of a patient's problems and start the best available treatment. A patient who poses a "diagnostic dilemma" for more than a few days is, well, exciting. Hardly anyone eludes diagnosis for a week. It took 10 days to get to a diagnosis for my patient, during which time he became a minor celebrity as everyone struggled to be the first to figure out what he had.

He turned out to have a rare condition called Sweet's syndrome, which is known to the few specialists who are familiar with it as febrile neutrophilic dermatosis. I had heard about this condition but had never seen it before. It is a skin disease in which white blood cells invade the skin, causing exquisite pain and tenderness. Its cause is unknown, but Sweet's syndrome tends to occur in patients with cancers or infections. It usually improves with high doses of steroids, as it did in the case of my patient.

However, before that diagnosis was made, the end of a month came and went, and that meant that my patient had changes in almost all of his many physicians. The schedules did not all change at the end of the month, as some of the physicians' schedules were in two-week blocks. But during my patient's 10-day admission, he had changes in his intern and resident physicians, the hospitalist who was his attending physician, and the consultation teams in rheumatology, infectious disease, and dermatology. He was never neglected—he was, after all, what we call a fascinoma—a fascinating case. In fact, he received so much attention that *both* of the rheumatologists who had treated him gave him appointments for office visits after the hospitalization.

It was at this point that my patient's wife e-mailed me, asking whether it was really necessary for him to see both rheumatologists. They lived an hour away, after all, and it was still a struggle for the patient to get into and out of bed, let alone a car. They would be happy to do it if it was important, but was it?

I was embarrassed by the confusion. I apologized and tried to put the best possible spin on it, saying that my colleagues had been overzealous in their efforts to make sure that his problems received appropriate follow-up after discharge from the hospital. It was at this point that the patient's wife wrote that she and her husband were "frightened"—she used that word—by the number of clinicians involved in her husband's care. She continued, "We are depending on you to tie all this together."

I am a hard worker, and I have not received too many reminders in my career to "do your job." But I recognized this one when it arrived. I described the case and the e-mail to my friend and colleague, the physician-writer Atul Gawande, and he said, "Patients like this one are a stress test for our healthcare system. They show us where and how we break down and fall apart."

In cardiology, when we do stress tests, patients ask whether they passed. Actually, no one passes or fails a stress test. The speed and the incline of the treadmill are increased bit by bit until the patient has to stop. Everyone has to stop eventually; the question is how soon and why. Cardiologists use stress tests to determine how long patients can keep going, how much they can push themselves, what makes them stop, and how their hearts are doing when they reach their limit.

Patients like mine unmask the breaking points of our health-care system: the points at which even smart, good, hardworking clinicians who are doing their best fail to inspire trust or give patients the peace of mind that comes from knowing that we are all working together on their behalf. It is ironic that the more sophisticated the care, the greater the risk for chaos—and the sense that patients are being forgotten.

What We've Lost

It wasn't always this way for either patients or clinicians. A century ago, the role model for all physicians was a doctor who prided himself on sitting at the bedside of patients and listening intently to what they had to say. That physician was Sir William Osler (1849–1919), a magnificent teacher who is often celebrated as the father of modern medicine and is frequently portrayed in photos and paintings surrounded by students as he sits in a chair at the bedside of patients.

Without exaggeration, Osler revolutionized medical education as the first physician in chief at Johns Hopkins Hospital by pulling medical trainees out of the lecture halls and onto hospital wards. Until then, students would earn medical degrees by attending classes taught by teachers with uncertain credentials. The poor quality of most of these schools was exposed in the landmark Flexner Report of 1910, in which Abraham Flexner described American medical education in harsh terms but praised a few institutions, most notably Johns Hopkins.

Medical training at Johns Hopkins was outstanding because Osler knew that even with the best teachers, classroom teaching did not prepare anyone to be a real physician. He believed that the only way to learn medicine was to see patients, listen to them, and thoroughly examine them. One of his most famous sayings was "If you listen carefully to the patient, they will tell you the diagnosis."

Figure 1.1.   William Osler at a patient's bedside. Reproduced by permission of the Osler Library of the History of Medicine, McGill University.

Osler would spend hours with students on teaching rounds at the bedsides of patients, demonstrating what could be discerned through thorough patient histories and physical examinations. Later, he would take students to the hospital morgue and perform autopsies so that they could correlate postmortem findings with what they had witnessed in living patients. He believed immersion with patients was so important that he established the first full-time live-in residency at Hopkins: a training period just after medical school when young physicians would reside in the hospital so that they could be around their patients constantly.

Osler knew that sitting by the bedside to give emotional comfort to patients was often the best thing physicians of his era could offer. Through countless hours of unflinchingly honest observations of patients, Osler could see that many treatments simply did not work. He was fond of quoting Oliver Wendell Holmes's quip that if all the medications that were used to treat patients were dumped into the ocean, it would be good for patients but very bad for fish. Instead, Osler advocated accurate diagnosis, followed by reliance on "mother rest and father time."[2]

Osler cited Hippocrates as saying that "for the physician to cultivate prognosis, and nothing so much inspires confidence as the power of foreseeing and foretelling in the presence of the sick the present, the past, and the future, he will indeed manage the cure best who has foreseen what is to happen."[3] In light of the lack of effective treatments, he believed that much of the real role of physicians consisted of predicting the patient's future and relieving the patient's suffering because he knew that in his era, physicians could only rarely change destiny.

The Era of Optimism

By 1919, when Osler died, a victim of the worldwide Spanish influenza epidemic, that fatalism was just about to start giving way to optimism. In the decade that followed, the first glimpses of truly effective treatments for diseases that had been routinely fatal began to emerge. In 1921, for example, insulin was extracted from animals by a Canadian researcher named Frederick Banting and his student Charles Best. A year later, they gave it to a boy dying from diabetes at Toronto General Hospital. The first injection nearly killed the boy because of an allergic reaction, and the scientists worked to purify the insulin. The second time they gave it, the results were miraculous. They went around a ward of children who were in comas because they were dying from diabetes and injected each child with the new insulin. By the time they were injecting the last child, the first was awakening.

In 1923, a surgeon at Harvard Medical School and Peter Bent Brigham Hospital named Elliott Cutler performed the first successful major heart operation, opening a narrowed valve in the heart of a 12-year-old girl. In 1928, Alexander Fleming observed that bacteria on a culture plate had been killed by a contaminating mold, leading to the discovery of penicillin. As it turned out, most of the research advances in the 1920s took decades to make a real difference in medical care. For example, Elliott Cutler's next several patients all died, and major heart surgery was not undertaken again until after World War II.

However, during that period, the culture of medicine began to change, a process that was captured in a Pulitzer Prize–winning novel published in 1925 by the American writer Sinclair Lewis. It was a book that approached required reading for young aspiring physicians. *Arrowsmith* tells the story of a bright young man who becomes a physician and researcher and makes discoveries that help curb an epidemic. His studies take Martin Arrowsmith from a small town to New York City. Along the way, Arrowsmith loses his wife to the epidemic he was studying, setting off a cycle of despair and preoccupation with superficial values such as wealth and fame. Eventually, however, Arrowsmith abandons New York and the fast life and resumes his research career in rural Vermont.

Arrowsmith reflected the hope and excitement that was beginning to surround medical research in the 1920s. Technical advances increasingly allowed scientists to measure processes at work inside the bodies of healthy people (physiology) and understand how those processes changed when diseases developed (pathophysiology). Insights into the mechanisms of diseases set the stage for treatments that might actually stop or reverse them.

World War II led to enormous investments in medical research. For example, the U.S. government funded studies of shock—the condition in which blood flow is inadequate to support normal organ function—in hopes of helping wounded soldiers survive. That research led to the development of cardiac catheterization, in which thin tubes are inserted into blood vessels and threaded into and around the heart. That innovation ultimately led to coronary angiography, coronary artery bypass graft surgery, and coronary angioplasty.

The desperate efforts to save wounded soldiers also led to a general increase in the audacity of physicians, especially surgeons. Cardiac surgery had gone into hibernation after Elliott Cutler's series of fatalities in the 1920s, but when soldiers arrived at hospitals in England with shrapnel buried in their beating hearts, surgeons such as Dwight Harken would not give up. Harken became famous for opening their hearts, pulling out the metal, and sewing the hearts up, and a surprising number of the soldiers he treated survived. Those experiences showed surgeons that it was possible to operate on the heart and set the stage for Harken and others to start performing heart valve surgery after the war.

There were also technical advances that had nothing to do with medicine, at least at first. Ultrasound was used to detect submarines in the sea and was eventually applied to detecting abnormalities in the body. Oscilloscopes became cardiac monitors. Research on the magnitude of g-forces that could be tolerated by fighter pilots before they lost consciousness provided new insights into cardiovascular physiology.

The cultural sequelae to the war also played a role in medical advances, especially in the United States, where people felt lucky to be alive and confident that they could take on any foe. A combination of gratitude and confidence led to an enormous increase in funding for research, and the fatalism that had characterized Osler's era gave way to optimism, even cockiness.

The transition that was under way after World War II is apparent in the first edition of what would become the bible of internal medicine, *Harrison's Principles of Internal Medicine.* The first edition was published in 1950, when the title did not yet include the name of its legendary editor, the cardiologist Tinsley R. Harrison. In the introduction, Harrison wrote, "The modern view of clinical teaching holds that the classic approach, with primary emphasis on specific diseases, is inadequate." He was announcing that there was a new era dawning in which physicians had to understand the science behind diseases because they might actually be able to do something other than hold patients' hands and predict their prognoses, as Osler had done.

However, in 1950, there were not many effective treatments yet. That first edition of *Harrison's* reflected a philosophical acceptance of death. Harrison, who wrote the cardiology chapters himself, reflected, "Arteriosclerosis, removing people from active life when the period of maximum fertility has passed, is of benefit to the young if it relieves them of the care of parents, or brings them an inheritance as they enter adult life. . . . Any attempts to eradicate such a disease from the urban population will be frustrated by natural selection and the survival of more grandchildren in families with few grandparents. Those best fitted to survive in a world growing more urban are those who cease to require support as soon as their roles as parents have been completed. Atherosclerosis and hypertension are now the chief factors in determining that we do not overstay our allotted span of life too long."[4]

Despite that fatalistic assessment, the book's emphasis on the scientific basis of disease helped foster a generation of physician-researchers who over the ensuing decades did more than predict the course of disease. They changed it. In Harrison's specialty, cardiology, the next 20 years would see the introduction of game-changing medications such as beta blockers and statins, both of which would decrease mortality by about one-third in large subsets of patients. Cardiopulmonary resuscitation (CPR) and cardiac defibrillation (the use of electric shocks to attempt to revert a life-threatening heart rhythm to normal) were both described in 1960, setting the stage for the development of the coronary care unit a few years later. Once it was possible to keep some patients alive after a cardiac arrest, there was a good reason to concentrate those patients in a place with the technology to save them and personnel trained in that technology.

Before the development of CPR and the coronary care unit, beepers were essentially unknown in medicine. Since not much could be done to save a dying patient, there was no particular need to rush to the patient's bedside. But in the new era, getting physicians to the bedside of patients within a few minutes might make the difference between life and death. The beeper quickly became a badge of honor for physicians. The little device conveyed the message "I might be needed somewhere at any moment."

Another change was the development of team care. Even with beepers, physicians couldn't be everywhere at once. Therefore, nurses in the coronary care units were trained and empowered to use defibrillators and start CPR without awaiting physicians' orders. Until then, the doctor had always been in charge and nothing happened without his (it was virtually always a man) issuance of an order. But now there was simply too much to do, and nurses were given the autonomy to decide whether to use certain lifesaving measures. The coronary care unit thus drove major advances for nurses and, by extension, for women and established the idea of teamwork in medicine.

More advances followed in rapid succession. The 1960s, 1970s, and 1980s saw the development of coronary angiography, coronary artery bypass graft surgery, coronary angioplasty, thrombolysis ("clot-busting" drugs that dissolve the blood clots that are the cause of most heart attacks and strokes), and a succession of other advances. These advances have extended the lives of and given hope to untold numbers of patients.

Cardiology wasn't the only field to experience seismic changes in the final decades of the twentieth century. In oncology, the development of chemotherapy enabled the treatment of systemic disease. Two previously fatal diseases of children and young adults—acute lymphoblastic leukemia and Hodgkin's lymphoma—became potentially curable, as did testicular cancer. The development of colonoscopy and mammography made it possible to screen for cancers of the colon and breast. Hospitals sprouted oncology wings and then cancer centers.

Technology was also transforming surgery. Miniaturized cameras and robotics made it possible to remove a gallbladder or cartilage fragments from a knee through a "Band-Aid" incision. Hip and knee replacements became common. Cataracts no longer meant impending blindness, only the need for a lens replacement.

The Downside of Progress

There are now a tremendous number of clinicians involved in delivering all this expertise, and their focus is often narrow. A study published in 2000 showed that the average Medicare patient saw seven different doctors per year and that those physicians were in four different medical practices, making it unlikely that they would interact directly with one another in the course of a day. Most of those physicians were specialists, and the question on their minds as they would see patients was often "Does this patient have something that will benefit from what I do?" as opposed to "What is wrong with this patient, and what does he or she need?"

The difference between these questions was brought home for me when I was struggling to take care of one of my patients, an aging MIT professor who had developed increasing difficulty walking and did not fit into any obvious disease category that I could identify. I sent him to a good neurologist, a good orthopedist, and a good rheumatologist who specialized in muscle diseases.

After the two months it took to get those consultations, the responses I received were "It is not his nerves," "It is not his joints," and "It is not his muscles." None of them told me what they thought his problem actually was or what we should do. Over time, I encountered each of those physicians in the hallway and mentioned my patient. They all had good ideas and were happy to contribute them, but until those face-to-face meetings, they had considered only the question "Is this what I do?"

Even when physicians recognize patients' real concerns, there is so much to do and so much to think about that their interactions feel hopelessly rushed. Studies show that the number of patient visits to physicians' offices has been steadily rising, with physicians squeezing increasing numbers of visits into their day. Despite this trend, the average time doctors spend with patients has gone up slightly, but there is so much more to discuss today than there was a generation ago that the time available for an office visit seems inadequate.

All too often, the cumulative effect from the patient's perspective is that too many clinicians are involved, each with a narrow focus and none who are looking at the big picture. In short, no doctor has all the information—or full accountability—for the patient's care, and neither the patients nor the doctors feel very good about this.

Making Sense of the Confusion

Many patients and families simply endure the confusion, but others cannot. An example of the latter is Suzanne House, whose 42-year-old husband, Jerry, died in 2008 at my hospital. He had been diagnosed with chronic lymphocytic leukemia five years earlier. Jerry House received six rounds of chemotherapy and was declared to be in remission just three months after he had been diagnosed with cancer.

That remission lasted for two and a half years. The cancer's return was diagnosed in May 2006, on the Houses' ninth wedding anniversary. Suzanne was six months pregnant with their third son. Over the next two years, Jerry endured a grueling series of chemotherapy treatments in preparation for a bone marrow transplant—his best chance for a cure. But in the summer of 2008, after a hospital stay of 43 days, he died from a combination of his cancer and infections that had attacked both of his lungs.

The last sentence is, of course, a dispassionate distillation of a prolonged nightmarish experience that remains vivid to Suzanne House even today. She still remembers new interns and residents speaking in voices that were "incredibly loud, asking mundane questions such as 'So when did you first think you may have leukemia, Mr. House?'" She recalls that her husband would look at her and shake his head in disbelief. After all, that information was in his voluminous medical record. Her sense was that every physician was starting from scratch. Their experience was, as she describes it, "All day long, different shifts, different residents, and loud, strange questions."

Everyone—and there were many types of experts involved—was trying his or her hardest to save Jerry House. Pulmonary, oncology, and infectious disease physicians came in and out several times a day, accompanied by residents and fellows, nurse practitioners, and social workers. Suzanne, an attorney, and Jerry's relatives peppered the clinicians with questions and hung on every word of the responses. Some physicians thought the problem was white blood cells from his cancer. Others thought it was a fungal infection. One said he was receiving the right medications to turn things around. Another said he might have only two weeks to live.

In retrospect, all those clinicians were mostly correct and were not really contradicting one another. There almost surely was cancer *and* infection in his lungs. He *was* receiving the "right" treatments. And their chances of saving Jerry House were minuscule. To the family, however, the various messages were confusing and sometimes contradictory.

Jerry's primary nurse understood Suzanne's distress and said, "We need to call a family meeting." Everyone involved in the case—well over a dozen physicians, nurses, and a social worker—was assembled in one room. Suzanne opened by saying, "Our family didn't need this meeting. You did. I need all of you on the same page. You are telling us different things, and it is scaring us."

All the constituencies in turn said what they thought was going on and what Jerry's likely prognosis was. There was still no absolute proof, but there was more consensus among them than had been apparent in the past. The House family took careful notes, asked questions, and shortly thereafter was introduced to the palliative care service.

Suzanne recalls now that she did not even know what palliative care meant at the time. It involves a consultation team that focuses on comfort for patients who are nearing the end of life. The team members are experts in relieving pain, shortness of breath, fear, and anxiety. Her husband died peacefully early in the morning of August 1, 2008, with only Suzanne in the room. It was the day he had been scheduled to receive a bone marrow transplant.

It's hard to say there is anything like a happy ending to a story like this, but here is how she described what happened next in an e-mail to me: "I stand up, kiss his forehead, pull up his sheet to the top of his chest and then say a prayer. I then buzz for the nurse. I walk and meet the aide at the door. I tell her he is gone. She looks over and says, 'No.' I say, 'Yes.' Then she hugs me and takes me down to the family room.

"The rest of the story is remarkable in that I was able to meet, talk with, and hug his oncologist. He told me he loved me. I got to play Monday morning quarterback with his nurse practitioner. All of Jerry's infusion nurses and staff came over to see me. We hugged and cried. It was an amazing morning. I was able to have closure that not many people get."

Suzanne became moderately famous within the healthcare system where I work as "the woman who called a family meeting because the doctors needed it." She spoke at one of our meetings, focusing on improving care of patients at the end of life, which is where we first met. At lunch after her talk, one of our neurosurgeons said to me that he completely understood how all of our colleagues had been doing their best but had created panic among the House family.

"To tell you the truth, I am embarrassed by what she described," he said. "The question is whether we are just going to leave this meeting and go back to the hospital and do things the same way."

That comment by that neurosurgeon brings us to one of the most puzzling and daunting aspects of the problem. With so many good people working so hard, why has healthcare been so resistant to change? Why haven't healthcare providers reorganized themselves to make disorganized and impersonal care a thing of the past?

The Problem with Healthcare Is People Like Me

I opened an article that I wrote in 2010 for the *Harvard Business Review* with the line "The problem with healthcare is people like me." I went on to describe how "people like me" include "doctors (mostly men) in our fifties and beyond, who learned medicine when it was more art and less finance. We were taught to go to the hospital before dawn, stay until our patients were stable, focus on the needs of each patient before us, and not worry about costs. We were taught to review every test result with our own eyes—to depend on no one. We were taught that the only way to ensure quality was to adopt high personal standards for ourselves and meet them.

"Now we are in charge. And that's a problem, because healthcare today needs a fundamentally different approach—and a new breed of leaders."[5]

My comments in that article were focused on physicians, but they pertain to other types of clinicians. We are demanding change from good, hardworking people who know that they are good and hardworking. These themes also affect the nonclinical personnel who may not deliver care themselves but influence patients' experiences: the front desk personnel, the people who address financial issues, the staff members who help patients get from one place to another. Healthcare today is a team sport; the good intentions and hard work of individuals cannot guarantee quality or efficiency. Healthcare today is also fast-paced and relentless. It is hard for anyone to be at his or her best all the time for every patient.

This challenge is exacerbated by a crisis in morale among many in healthcare, especially clinicians. A generation ago, being a doctor or nurse meant having a secure job and the respect of the community, but today neither income nor status is guaranteed. Much of the discussion about the angst among healthcare providers focuses on financial issues, but even if there were no financial challenges, there would still be a need for change and there would still be anxiety among healthcare providers about what that change implies.

The term that is used with increasing frequency to describe this crisis in morale is *burnout*. Burnout is characterized by "a low sense of personal accomplishment, emotional exhaustion, cynicism and depersonalization."[6] As one leading researcher noted, burnout starts when "energy turns into exhaustion, involvement turns into cynicism, and efficacy turns into ineffectiveness."[7] The net effect: many clinicians and others in healthcare feel weary from the struggle to get through the day, and they despair about their ability to make a difference in the problems of individual patients, let alone the overall challenges facing healthcare.

The notion that clinicians could say they are "burned out" may seem startling at first to people in other fields. After all, clinicians do some of the most respected work in society, are well compensated, and are the recipients of positive feedback when they do the most routine tasks. (Patients commonly begin their visits with "Thank you for seeing me.") But data reliably show that 25 to 60 percent of physicians, nurses, and other medical personnel report burnout.

In a 2015 study, 5,404 healthcare personnel were asked the question: "Overall, based on your definition of burnout, how would you rate your level of burnout?" They were instructed to answer by using the following scale:

"I enjoy my work. I have no symptoms of burnout."	1
"Occasionally I am under stress, and I don't always have as much energy as I once did, but I don't feel burned out."	2
"I am definitely burning out and have one or more symptoms of burnout, such as physical and emotional exhaustion."	3
"The symptoms of burnout that I'm experiencing won't go away. I think about frustration at work a lot."	4
"I feel completely burned out and often wonder if I can go on. I am at the point where I may need some changes or may need to seek some sort of help."	5

More than 38 percent of the respondents answered 3, 4, or 5 and were classified as having burnout. The burnout rates were highest in those with the most clinical involvement with patients, but even clerks had a 35 percent burnout rate.[8]

Burnout is believed to result from a range of growing internal and external pressures. There is so much more to do and to worry about. There are so many more people with whom to try to coordinate one's work. There is so much more pressure to do everything quickly and efficiently.

A generation ago, doctors and nurses rarely were evaluated. Today, they receive constant feedback that their efforts are insufficient. Whatever aggravations characterize work as a clinician today, the future seems likely to hold even more. The loss of certainty about their professional lives is sinking in, and clinicians are going through something akin to the stages of grief. As Toby Cosgrove, the CEO of Cleveland Clinic, and I wrote in an article in 2014,[9] few are still in the denial phase, and many have moved to the next phase: anger.

As Cosgrove and I wrote, there is really only one solution to this angst among clinicians. We have to focus on what everyone agrees trumps all of our concerns as individuals: what is happening to patients. We have to persuade our colleagues to focus on the suffering of our patients with the well-founded hope and expectation that our colleagues will rise to the challenge of relieving it.

2 | The Imperative

CREATING AN EPIDEMIC of empathy is not an act of charity. It is a strategic business imperative. For many healthcare organizations, pursuing this goal is actually a stay-in-business decision because we are entering an era in which the healthcare marketplace is driven by competition based on value. In this marketplace, the healthcare providers who can organize their personnel to deliver high-quality care with efficiency and empathy will be the ones that thrive. In contrast, the providers who are unable to move their personnel into new models of working together to meet patients' needs may watch their patient-service revenue erode as competitors take their patients away.

This new competitive environment represents a clear break from a past in which care was organized around maximizing the volume of healthcare services. This historical orientation was not a reflection of moral weakness; the assumption was that those services were almost always beneficial for patients and that the more that was done, the more patients would benefit. However, that orientation has ceased to be viable in a world where resources are limited and where a healthcare system with complex capabilities frequently does not benefit patients and sometimes causes harm.

Why We Resist Change

If there are still some healthcare leaders who do not believe that fundamental change is under way, their numbers are dwindling with each passing year. The skepticism that remains stems from decades of hearing that a revolution is about to occur in healthcare yet realizing a few years later that not much has changed. Healthcare continues to be organized around what physicians do, and their activities still continue to be rewarded through the fee-for-service systems.

Is there any reason to believe anything will be different this time? Why should physicians disrupt the lives of their colleagues by asking them to reorganize their care? They remember the 1990s, when similar speculations that the healthcare system was about to change were commonly made. They thus hesitate to anger colleagues by asking them to work differently or reduce their incomes by performing fewer services.

They say that terms such as *value* and *patient-centered* may sound good but are only abstractions that are difficult to apply when it comes to actual healthcare delivery. They express doubts that patients can make the best decisions about their own care because they do not have physicians' and nurses' intimate knowledge of medicine. They look skeptically at individual measures of quality and highlight potential flaws. ("What about Dr. Adams? He scores high in patient satisfaction, but we all know he is completely out of date.")

In the absence of measurement systems that capture what they consider quality, they fall back on something traditional: trust that doctors know what they are doing. They believe that what healthcare providers do is predominantly good, and they know that the services they provide are valued by patients and their families. Why else would hospitals and physician offices be so full? They think of all the exceptions that undermine any existing quality measure and argue that the most important step in preserving quality is to protect the autonomy of physicians. After all, doctors are the ones who understand medicine, and no one should make it difficult for them to do whatever they consider the best thing for any specific patient.

There is one more nuance to their resistance to the possibility that change is afoot. Money currently flows on the basis of the volume of services provided rather than through alternative approaches that reward providers on the basis of whether they have met patients' needs. In any large healthcare organization, the livelihoods of thousands of people depend on steady cash flow that stops the instant there is a decline in services reimbursed by fee-for-service contracts. That cash flow is similarly diminished by every service that is not directly compensated, such as an extra phone call to make sure that a patient is not unduly frightened before or after surgery. Despite the high volume of care delivered, the financial margins of most healthcare organizations are so thin that any change threatens major disruption. The loss of a million dollars in revenue means that 10 people will lose their jobs, maybe more. In this context, it seems irresponsible to rock the boat.

Why This Time Is Different

The basic dynamics of the healthcare marketplace are changing in irreversible ways. In the old days, patients could go almost anywhere for their care with minimal if any impact on their personal costs. Not surprisingly, their choice of providers was based on some combination of reputation and convenience. If providers had enough patients, they became indispensable to health insurance plans and to employers who did not want to anger patients who were loyal to their healthcare providers. Those providers could then negotiate contracts that covered all their costs, including costs for uninsured patients and patients covered by Medicare or Medicaid who brought in less revenue than the cost of their care.

Today, however, some of the decisions that will determine the viability of healthcare organizations do not occur at the contract table where agreements with insurance companies are reached. Nor do they occur at conference tables of employers who are deciding which insurance products to offer. The decisions are being made at kitchen tables in the homes of people who are struggling to stretch their budgets to meet their expenses. Those budgets are based on incomes that have been essentially flat or even declining. Healthcare costs are rising less steeply than they did in the past, but they still seem to be rising faster than the incomes of most households. In 2013, healthcare spending increased 3.6 percent[1] whereas the median household income increased only 0.6 percent,[2] which means net buying power went down.

So what's new? Those families now have another option besides cutting other expenses or going deeper into debt: they can choose a less expensive health plan. Many employers offered only one, two, or three options in the past, and the distinctions were often subtle at best. However, the trend is toward employers offering more options, including lower-cost plans in which employees decide whether they want to trade access to all providers for lower costs. In short, more and more people are factoring cost into the way they choose providers. They are choosing insurance products that they can afford and then searching for the best care available within their options.

Another important trend is that larger employers and health plans are steering patients toward institutions with which they have "bundled payment" contracts in which the providers deliver episodes of care for a set fee. For example, employers such as Walmart, Lowe's, and General Electric are sending employees who need major heart surgery to Cleveland Clinic, Geisinger Health System, and other providers that have agreed to a fixed price and also have excellent quality records.

As a result, value is starting to influence where patients go for primary care, radiology tests, colonoscopies, cardiac surgeries, and other procedures. Although relatively few patients are changing where they get their care, the loss of only a small percentage of patients is enough to destabilize a hospital or physician group. Providers now realize that they need to hold on to their patients because if they lose their market share, they are at risk of going out of business no matter how well their contracts reimburse them.

Competing on Value

In one important marketplace, Florida, competition is leading to better and more efficient care. Florida's warm winters attract elderly retirees who are tired of shoveling snow and braving freezing rain. The 12 U.S. counties with the highest percentage of citizens over age 65 are in Florida. Virtually all these patients are covered by Medicare, which does not pay hospitals or physicians as much as most commercial insurance plans do.

In the past, hospitals and doctors would take care of Medicare patients, but from a financial perspective they were better off when commercial patients filled hospital beds and office-visit schedules. The providers could negotiate higher payments from the commercial insurers and use the profits to cover their losses from taking care of Medicare patients. That dynamic worked well for many providers until recently.

Now commercial insurers are responding to pressures to control costs from employers and are refusing to raise payments enough to allow providers to do business as usual. In fact, many insurers are demanding cuts in their payments to providers. Unable to cross-subsidize the care of Medicare patients, hospitals and doctor groups could decide to take fewer elderly patients. However, without Medicare beneficiaries, they wouldn't have the critical mass of patients they need for either high quality or efficiency. Providers have realized that they need to hold on to their elderly patients and also figure out how to care for them efficiently so that they can at least break even if they accept Medicare's levels of payment.

The first step in retaining or increasing their market share of the elderly is to mount focused efforts to meet the needs of that population. As one hospital leader told me, "I wake up every day wondering how I can get elderly patients—who have a hard time getting around to begin with—to drive past a hospital near their home and come to me. The only way to make that happen is to do a great job for them."

Sarasota Memorial Hospital has reached out to seniors by creating an outlet in a major mall. Although no medical care is delivered there, the hospital sponsors guided walks through the mall, followed by educational sessions. Sarasota Memorial is attracting and serving elderly patients by meeting their needs for information and exercise. It is being rewarded by an increasing market share because many of the elderly who take mall walks are deciding to seek care from Sarasota Memorial clinicians.

This dynamic, in which providers first compete for patients by meeting their needs and then work to lower costs enough to earn a margin, is good for society but stressful for providers. Even though healthcare providers in general and physicians in particular tend to be competitive (they all want to be "the best"), they don't enjoy waiting to see whether their hard work is going to be rewarded. Nevertheless, the alternatives to a marketplace driven by competition—for example, shifting costs to patients or trying to use government regulation to control costs and ensure quality—are not pretty for patients or providers.

Accordingly, many providers are changing the way they work in preparation for a marketplace driven by competition. For example, Cleveland Clinic publishes its clinical outcomes for a widening array of medical and surgical conditions, and University of Utah Healthcare publishes online all of its patients' comments—good, bad, and ugly. In the old marketplace, where reputation was what mattered most, why would any healthcare organization publish anything negative about its care? In the new one, where providers are starting to compete on value for patients, organizations such as Cleveland Clinic and the University of Utah have figured out that they gain an advantage by putting their results before the public, thus motivating their own personnel to improve the care they provide.

Real competition challenges some of the traditional ways in which clinicians think about what constitutes excellence. In many organizations around the country, I have met good, hardworking doctors who take justifiable pride in quality metrics such as the reliability with which they deliver evidence-based medicine, for example, whether they give beta blockers to a patient after acute myocardial infarction or how long it takes them to get a patient with a heart attack from the emergency department to the cardiac catheterization laboratory.

The work needed to make progress on such measures should not be trivialized, but the fact is that patients assume that providers are going to be reliable in delivering evidence-based processes. They are not particularly interested in the difference between 97 percent reliability and 99 percent reliability in the performance of such processes, and they should not be. Instead, they base their choices about where to go on what is *different* among providers, and these traditional quality metrics are often all too similar.

Providers facing competition need a competitive differentiator, and that requires the development of a real strategy.

The Strategic Imperative: Improving Value for Patients

What does strategy really mean? As Michael Porter and I wrote in the *New England Journal of Medicine*, strategy is something fundamentally different from operational effectiveness. Operational effectiveness means working hard, embracing best practices, and burnishing reputations that attract both patients and talent. Those good management practices remain absolutely essential; in fact, they are the table stakes for providers. Even if they have the most brilliant strategy in the world, they will not be successful without excellent operational effectiveness.

But these days, operational effectiveness is no longer a guarantee of success. To thrive, providers today also need strategy, which is about making the choices necessary to distinguish an organization in meeting customers' needs. Choices are painful; they anger constituents who feel that they are losing out. To make choices, providers need to address some challenging issues.

The first and most fundamental question, as we wrote in our *New England Journal of Medicine* paper, is "What is our goal?" Strategy begins with clarity on this most basic question. The answer must be understood throughout the organization and used to guide all decision making. There is no goal that serves healthcare organizations as well as does improving value for patients. It is the one aim that all stakeholders embrace.[3]

Why is clarity on this seemingly obvious point important? First, many healthcare organizations have evolved with multiple missions in mind, such as serving their communities, teaching, and doing research. Individually, every one of these goals is laudable and important. Collectively, they constitute a mishmash in which it is difficult or impossible to make decisions about how scarce resources are allocated. To guide decision making in a time of turmoil, we think one goal—improving value for patients—must be the clear top priority. The other goals should be pursued but be subordinated to value for patients.

The other reason for achieving clarity on the goal is that many organizations have misconceptions about what strategy really means. For example, achieving a specific financial margin target such as 3 percent is not a strategy. Growing or merging with other organizations is not a strategy. Adding the infrastructure for new technologies is not a strategy. These decisions and results may flow from strategy, but they are not strategy itself. They do not directly define *what* the organization is trying to do for *whom*.

Providers that understand that their goal is to improve value for patients can then organize themselves to meet patients' needs and become more efficient in doing so. This strategy will be robust regardless of whether they are being paid a fee for service or are reimbursed according to some other model. Providers are going to be living with a mixed payment model forever, and this means that their strategy—their core understanding of what they are trying to do for whom—must transcend the payment model.

Improving value for patients fills the bill. Contracting is important, of course, on a year-to-year basis, but over the long haul the success of providers will be determined by their ability to improve value for patients. If providers can produce better outcomes, they will attract more patients. Greater efficiency will improve financial margins. Just as important, they will be more successful in retaining personnel, who are always influenced by the extent to which they feel pride in their place of work.

The Business Imperative: Patient Loyalty and Market Share

If the strategic imperative for healthcare organizations is to meet patients' needs effectively and efficiently, just what are those needs? As a practicing physician, I know that I have good insight—often the *best* insight—into the medical needs of my patients, such as what tests they need to screen for disease and what treatments may help them the most. As important as those clinical issues may be, however, they do not constitute the totality of healthcare. Other factors are important in determining where patients are going to go for their care and influence whether they will stay there.

Not so long ago, patient loyalty was a nice-to-have for healthcare providers. Today, it is fast becoming a life-or-death issue. In last century's version of the fee-for-service system, whether patients returned for care did not really matter financially as long as there were other patients to take their place. Of course, no hospital or doctor wanted to disappoint patients, but if a practice had a long waiting list for appointments or if a hospital's bed occupancy was high, no one worried too much if some patients decided to get their care elsewhere.

That casual perspective toward patient loyalty changed with the passage of the Affordable Care Act in 2010. For more and more Americans each year, insurance products provide incentives to obtain care from limited networks of providers. Many patients are pausing to weigh their loyalty to their current physicians or hospitals against the impact on their household budgets of staying with those providers. Some are changing providers as a result.

Many providers are participating in accountable care organization (ACO) contracts, in which they bear responsibility for the total cost of care of a patient population. For ACO providers, it is important to hold on to all patients, healthy as well as sick, and to keep those patients' care within their organization. To do so, they need to meet their patients' needs and give them peace of mind that those needs are being met.

What, besides out-of-pocket costs, is likely to influence patients as they choose where to get healthcare? They want providers to work together and work with them to help them live lives that are as long and healthy as possible. They want peace of mind that their outcomes are as good as they can be even though they may fall short of perfect health.

These concerns are reflected in Figure 2.1, which summarizes an analysis of nearly a million surveys of patients, identifying factors that separate patients into groups with different levels of commitment to their clinicians and their medical practices. In

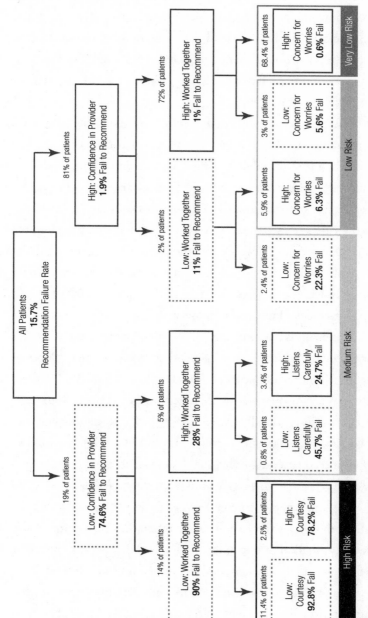

Figure 2.1　What drives patient loyalty

this analysis, "Recommendation Failure Rate" is the percentage of patients who did not give a top rating on a 5-point scale when asked how likely they were to recommend either the provider or the practice (15 percent overall). The likelihood of recommending a practice is a reasonable (and probably the best available) reflection of the extent to which patients have peace of mind that their care is optimizing their outcomes.

The most important single variable in driving the likelihood to recommend is the patient's confidence in the clinician. But even when that confidence is high (see the right side of the decision tree), the Recommendation Failure Rate rises to 11 percent if patients did not think that everyone was working well together on their behalf and to 22.3 percent if they felt that the care provider team was not deeply concerned about their issues (bottom row, fourth box from the right). The algorithm can be used to compare physicians on the percentages of their patients who fall into high-, medium-, low-, and very low risk groups.

This analysis is interesting not just for what is included but also for the factors that were *not* included after taking the variables in the decision tree into account. Variables that did not add statistically important information included waiting time, convenience, and amenities. Naturally, patients do not want to wait longer than necessary, but what is most important in influencing their likelihood of recommending physician practices is having good clinicians who listen to their issues and work well together.

The same themes emerge from analyses of patient-experience data from people who have been hospitalized, which demonstrate that coordination of care and communication are most important in driving patients' likelihood of recommending an institution. The single most important driver is nursing communication with the patient; this makes sense because nurses do so much of the actual work with patients during their hospitalizations and play an enormous role in conveying to patients what is happening and what will happen next. Variables such as food and parking rank at the very bottom of virtually all analyses of what drives patients' likelihood to recommend hospitals.

Similarly, in analyses of survey responses from emergency department patients, the most important factors driving patients' likelihood of recommending the facility are whether they feel that the staff cares about them, whether they feel the staff has kept them informed about delays and what is happening, and whether they feel they have been treated with courtesy. Issues such as pain control and actual waiting time were not statistically important after taking into account whether the clinicians demonstrated empathy and communicated well with patients.

The same themes emerge in analyses of the pediatric population and every other segment of patients where my colleagues and I have looked. Patients want good clinicians who are working well together and are listening to them. Those themes make sense to clinicians and certainly do not clash with what drew them to healthcare. The bottom line is that healthcare is in the fortunate position of having a business imperative that resonates well with the values of its personnel.

The Clinical Imperative: Reliability and Improvement

The strategic imperative for healthcare providers in this new era of value-driven competition is to meet patients' needs as effectively and efficiently as possible. The business imperative that logically flows from meeting patients' needs is to provide care that inspires confidence in clinicians as individuals but is also coordinated and empathic. That all sounds good, but what do these imperatives translate into for doctors, nurses, and other frontline caregivers?

Imperatives are far from welcome to many clinicians and other personnel who are already under considerable duress. As is true in every business sector, healthcare personnel are struggling with constant pressures to do more and do it better with fewer resources. These pressures are especially daunting in healthcare because of its complexity: there are so many issues to address and so many definitions of "better."

The result of the complexity of healthcare is that dozens, even hundreds, of metrics are being used to evaluate healthcare providers, and their cumulative weight can be overwhelming. The performance report cards in many organizations are literally hundreds of pages long, with data on mortality, complications, compliance with clinical guidelines, safety events, patient experience, and financial issues. In many organizations dozens of personnel are employed just to collect, analyze, and report these data.

The many different performance metrics can, paradoxically, impede improvement. Measurement overload is a common complaint. "Just tell me three things you want me to do, and I'll do them," one physician said to me recently. "But if you tell me twenty-five things, it is going to be hard for me to pay attention to any of them."

In fact, there are really just two things healthcare providers need to focus on: The first is to be *reliable* in delivering care the way it should be delivered, which means excellent technical quality, coordination, empathy, and efficiency. The second is making *improvement* a perpetual focus. Providers should never be satisfied with their care as it is. There are always ways in which they can improve; no one should ever consider himself or herself the best or even good enough.

Performance measurement is still fairly new in healthcare. For simplicity's sake, the cultural history of healthcare performance improvement can be divided into the eras before and after the 2000 publication of *To Err Is Human* by the Institute of Medicine (IOM).[4] Before the report, the conventional wisdom was that the quality of healthcare in the United States was generally excellent but difficult to measure. Guidelines had been developed for some topics, but in the absence of alternatives, the preservation of physicians' autonomy to do what they judged best for patients was often invoked as the first principle of high-quality healthcare.

In truth, most healthcare providers knew well before 1999 that healthcare often fell short of what it could and should have been. But *To Err Is Human* and its 2001 successor, *Crossing the Quality Chasm*,[5] drew attention to gaps in safety, reliability, efficiency, and the overall experience of care. At many institutions, the work of improving healthcare quality and efficiency was broken down into various subcategories, leading to several new roles and an abundance of new metrics. New titles included chief quality officer, chief safety officer, chief patient experience officer, chief population management officer, and chief value officer. Inevitably, complaints about measurement fatigue and skepticism about performance measurement emerged.[6]

Research and experience in subsequent years have shown that all these streams of work are important and none can be ignored. The implication is that it is time to reintegrate the various streams of quality that emerged after the IOM reports: reliability in adherence to guidelines, safety, patient experience, and efficiency. The basic challenge for healthcare providers is nothing less than to be reliably excellent in all of them.

The unsurprising reality is that no one is the best at everything and everyone has room for improvement on something. No institution can rest on its laurels because it has a fabulous reputation. We cannot assume that a hospital that is excellent on guideline compliance metrics is also excellent in patient safety. All the dimensions of quality are separate yet intertwined, and they combine to determine the outcomes and costs of care.

An important implication is that providers have to measure actual outcomes. Traditionally, clinicians have been leery of putting too much weight on patient outcomes such as mortality, other clinical outcomes, or patient experience because of difficulties with risk adjustment and the impact of clinical and socioeconomic factors beyond their control. That said, the real issue in healthcare is how patients are doing, not the reliability of providers. It is hard to improve if the focus is not on the real target.

No single outcome tells the story for any subset of patients. There are multiple outcomes that matter, and the fact is that they should all be measured and reported. Porter has described a hierarchy of outcomes, with Tier 1 outcomes (hard clinical outcomes) being the most important.[7] However, he argues, Tier 2 outcomes related to the processes of care (e.g., readmissions and the disutility of care) matter as well, as do Tier 3 outcomes, which reflect the durability of health interventions, such as the likelihood of a patient needing a repeat procedure. (There is more on this topic in Chapter 4.)

If an institution is statistically worse than expected on Tier 1 outcomes such as mortality, the data should precipitate an all-hands-on-deck effort to dissect whether patient selection, poor guideline adherence, or suboptimal safety is causing the gap. However, organizations cannot expect to pull away from the crowd on the basis of the hardest Tier 1 outcomes such as survival because other good organizations are likely to have similarly excellent mortality data. Attention should then be turned to other clinical outcomes, including patients' experience of care.

In summary, the strategic imperative for healthcare organizations reflects the demands of a healthcare marketplace increasingly driven by competition to create value for patients. To hold on to and increase their market shares, providers need to deliver coordinated and compassionate care. And to provide such care, providers must be reliable and constantly seek to improve their outcomes and costs.

These strategic, business, and clinical imperatives complement one another, but they are all disruptive for healthcare providers. The stakes are high because failure to respond makes it likely that organizations will fail to compete. They will lose market share and lose personnel to other organizations with better business prospects and higher morale.

The truth is that virtually everyone in healthcare wants to provide compassionate and coordinated care, and most clinicians recognize and admire such care when they see it. The question is how to drive its spread, and that process begins with a deeper understanding of what "it" is.

3 | The Response:
Empathy

WE KNOW THE problem: Over the last century, medical progress has taken fatalism out of medicine but has introduced chaos to the care of many patients and narrowed the focus of most clinicians. Doctors and nurses are working harder than ever at what they perceive to be their jobs, but many are getting less satisfaction from that work, and patients often feel lost in the shuffle.

We understand the imperative for healthcare providers to address the problem. We are entering a new healthcare marketplace that is being driven by competition that is based on value: meeting the needs of patients as efficiently as possible. To meet those needs, providers must be reliable in giving excellent care that is supported by evidence and doing it safely. However, such reliability is table stakes in modern healthcare. With competition in the air, reliability in technical quality is absolutely essential to be in the game but not enough to ensure success.

Thriving in the new healthcare marketplace requires more than physicians complying with guidelines. Patients want good clinicians who work well together and understand their patients' worries and concerns. Patients want coordinated and empathic care. They want to trust their individual clinicians and the organizations in which those clinicians work.

Organizations that can meet these needs and do so efficiently have the best chance of increasing their market share and retaining good personnel. The personnel in those organizations can have their cake and eat it, too: enjoy business success as well as professional pride. In fact, healthcare organizations should recognize that they can no longer have one without the other. They should also recognize that they can have both by delivering coordinated, empathic care.

Why Empathy Is Essential

The word *empathy* is really quite new, dating to the early twentieth century. It was coined by the psychologist Edward Titchener from two Greek roots: *em* ("in") and *pathos* ("feeling"). Titchener's aim was to translate the German term *Einfühlung*, or "feeling into," which was used in the study of aesthetics to describe a response to a work of art. It was subsequently extended to describe responses to living creatures as well. Just as people could feel into a Beethoven symphony or a Renoir painting, they could feel into their child's disappointment or a friend's grief.

As contemporary psychologists and philosophers have drilled more deeply into the concept, subclasses of empathy have emerged. In his bestseller *Emotional Intelligence,* the psychologist Daniel Goleman discusses three kinds of empathy: *Cognitive* empathy is the ability to understand what another person is experiencing. *Emotional* empathy is the ability to feel what another person is feeling. *Empathic* concern is the ability to sense what another person needs from you.

This is the trifecta that is sought and expected in healthcare, and clinicians are supposed to manifest all three. That is why I compare empathic care to dancing. The clinician has to pay attention to his or her partner in this dance, but selectively. Dancers who try to respond to every blink of the partner's eye are likely to lose the beat and become exhausted. If all doctors picked up every feeling in every one of their patents, they would burn out pretty quickly. Fortunately, empathic care doesn't require the full trifecta and that degree of emotional synchrony in every case. Cognitive empathy is adequate—or at least a good start—in most clinical situations. For example, patients are more interested in clinicians understanding that they are afraid than in having clinicians actually experience their fear.

The hazards of actually trying to feel what a patient is feeling are particularly powerful in psychiatry, in which clinicians have to learn to convey empathy while protecting themselves against getting swept into their patients' emotional maelstroms. In a 2007 essay in the *New York Times,* the psychiatrist Richard A. Friedman described having to explain to patients how he could imagine their pain even though he hadn't suffered clinical depression or experienced the death of a spouse as they had. "In the end, empathy is what makes it possible for us to read each other. And it is the reason your doctor can understand your problem without actually having to live it," he concluded.[1]

Friedman was right. We all do this all the time, often unconsciously. We understand our spouse's stress and frustration; we tap into our kids' excitement; we celebrate a friend's promotion with him or her; we know how hard it is for our aging parents to give up the family house for assisted living. This type of empathy is the glue that holds families together and cements social relationships.

Extending empathy to people we don't know or don't like is less natural and takes greater effort, but humans have been implored to do this perhaps since the dawn of civilization. Empathy is espoused by most religions as some version of the Golden Rule: treat others as you would like to be treated. Philosophers as varied as Plato,

Thomas More, and Adam Smith invoked something that resembles what we think of as empathy in their doctrines for society.

Healthcare providers will benefit from doing the same thing. Three sets of insights are useful in transforming empathy from a vague concept to a focus of healthcare strategy. The first is that empathy has a verified biological basis. The second is that empathy can be a cognitive process. The third is the acknowledgment that empathy can be eroded by distraction and stress and regained with a little work. In short, empathy is not a reflection of how good people may be but of how willing they are to be good.

The Biological Basis of Empathy

Sociologists have hypothesized that we are hardwired for empathy, probably because it is essential to the survival of our species. It drives us to care for infants and help others through rough patches. Households, businesses, and military units function better when their members have empathy for one another. Like two other essentials for survival—food and sex—empathy makes us feel good.

Neuroscience gives support to that theory. A series of experiments in the last decade has identified neurons in the inferior frontal and posterior parietal regions of the human brain that are active both when one is performing a task and when one is watching another person performing that task. Functional magnetic resonance imaging (fMRI) scans have shown that the same regions of the brain—dubbed the mirror neuron system—are active in people relaying an experience and those who are merely hearing about it. Mirror neurons may be at work when a mother's smile elicits a smile in her baby or when an outbreak of yawning erupts in a staff meeting.

A few years ago researchers took on the work of determining how contagious yawning originates and spreads. In one experiment, people yawned while undergoing fMRI scans and researchers noted their brain activity. When a second group of people was shown images of yawning people while being scanned, not only did the same regions of their brains light up, but the subjects yawned in response.

Although babies haven't been subjected to fMRI scans to test their mirror neuron activity, behavioral studies have determined that they begin to develop empathy early in infancy. Emotional contagion comes first. That is why babies seem to smile back at grinning adults. There is also evidence that infants begin to express cognitive empathy—attempting to comfort siblings who are crying—even before their first birthdays.

My colleague from Harvard Medical School Helen Riess, MD, has described how physiologic changes detectable through advanced imaging technologies demonstrate real resonance between patients and empathic clinicians.[2] The very regions of the brain that are activated in suffering patients are active in the physicians who care for them, although less intensely. This milder version of experiencing another person's pain may enable the observer to understand a person's distress without being overwhelmed by it.

Other research has shown that heart rate and skin conductance change when empathic relationships are at work. The bottom line from these various researchers is that empathy is real; it is based in neurobiology and is not a reflection of how good a person one is.

Empathy as a Cognitive Process

A second major useful insight about empathy is that it is ultimately based on thinking rather than feeling. In his book *Empathy in Patient Care*, Mohammadreza Hojat from Thomas Jefferson University describes empathy as "a predominantly *cognitive* (rather than emotional) attribute that involves an *understanding* (rather than feeling) of experiences, concerns and perspectives of the patient, combined with a capacity to *communicate* this understanding."[3]

Hojat draws a useful distinction between empathy and sympathy, which he describes as an emotional response, for example, feeling bad that a patient is enduring pain and suffering. Empathy has its roots in sympathy, of course, but it does more. Empathy enables clinicians to take actions that address the patient's concerns. At the end of the day, patients don't really want clinicians to *feel* badly about their pain (sympathy); they want clinicians to *understand* that they are in pain (empathy) and do something about it.

In the last 20 years we've seen what using cognitive empathy can accomplish on a global level. The Truth and Reconciliation Commission in South Africa brought together people with seemingly insurmountable prejudices to engage in an ongoing dialogue through which they have come to better understand one another's perspectives on apartheid. We have seen the recognition of same-sex marriage in most U.S. states and in nations as disparate as Uruguay and Ireland.

These watershed societal changes weren't accomplished by enforcing abstract principles but because humans met face-to-face and got to know "the other" personally. Political scientists have noted that the work of the Truth and Reconciliation Commission was most successful in smaller villages and towns where the participants—whatever their ethnicity—were known to one another. The same is true for same-sex marriage. These days, it seems almost clichéd to hear people say that their resistance to same-sex marriage was broken down when they got to know a gay couple in their neighborhood or understood that their own child was homosexual.

The participants in these dialogues didn't come to feel like people of a different race or sexual orientation, but they came to better understand how those people felt through hearing their stories. They acquired cognitive empathy by focusing on others and thinking about what they were seeing and hearing. They had to work at it.

The Work of Empathy

The realization that empathy can be acquired by working at it is good news, of course. After all, none of us is perfect, and it is hard to drive social change by urging everyone to become a better person. I daresay that most of us in healthcare are not lazy, and we are ready to work hard if we understand the task at hand.

In their memorable paper on empathy as emotional labor, Eric Larson and Xin Yao described empathy as "a psychological process that encompasses a collection of affective, cognitive, and behavioral mechanisms and outcomes in reaction to the observed experiences of another."[4] That description wasn't what made the paper memorable for me, however.

The authors address the "verb"—what it really means to build empathy and deliver empathic care. They write, "To cultivate an acute ability to empathize with others, one needs patience, curiosity, and willingness to subject one's mind to the patient's world. However, there are many obstacles that contemporary physicians face as they aspire to develop empathy." (They describe the distractions of modern life in healthcare and the lack of training that clinicians receive in the delivery of empathic care.)

But what really captured my attention was this statement: "We believe that better understanding of empathy—and more importantly, framing the psychological and behavioral activities in this process as acting methods used in emotional labor—would help physicians successfully incorporate empathy in their daily practice."

"Acting methods"? The phrase gave me pause when I first read this paper. Doctors as actors? I worried that this comparison might seem demeaning to many of my colleagues. But I thought about how, when I am about to walk into a room where a patient waits, I often stand for an instant and take a deep breath before entering, much as I imagine an actor does before striding onto the stage. And then I play my role.

I have long wondered how stage actors are able to play their roles night after night without feeling stale and pondered whether that consistency is akin to the consistency needed in healthcare. Patients—and audiences—want to see the stars at their best. I've spoken to some actors about this, and they tell me that their work is not just about reciting lines and making facial expressions but about reading and responding to the emotions of other actors onstage. That is how they never go stale.

In their article, Larson and Yao trace the concept of emotional labor to the service industry, in which workers who deal with the public are encouraged to display emotions consonant with the goals of their employer. In a sense, we all perform emotional labor when we are asked to reflect the ethos of a group to which we may belong but with which we may not be fully engaged. An example would be a person who has no interest in football being expected to cheer wildly for the local team.

Emotional labor can begin as acting in which one person observes the facial expression and body language of another. The observer then extrapolates what the other person might be thinking or feeling and tries to mirror that thought or emotion. With repetition, the observer actually begins to appreciate the other person's feelings and exhibits true empathy. The observers fake it until they become it.

The amount of emotional labor it takes to achieve empathy depends on the situation. For most people, it's not difficult to empathize with someone who is a lot like oneself. For example, a white middle-class emergency physician may find it easier to empathize with a bicycle commuter who was struck by a car while riding home from her job than with a homeless man who was hit by a car while walking on the same street.

Larson and Yao describe two types of emotional labor: surface acting and deep acting. The first has more in common with developing communication skills such as making eye contact, repeating the patient's statements, and responding appropriately. The second requires imagining the patient's emotional reaction and recalling a similar emotional experience of one's own. In a sense, surface acting is faking an emotional display by imitating facial expressions and the like. Deep acting involves drawing on one's own experiences to understand the emotions of another person.

For example, that doctor in the emergency department may never be able to fully grasp what it means to be homeless but can try to recall situations in which he felt desperate and without options even if the contexts are trivial in comparison with homelessness (e.g., how it felt to be stranded in an airport at night when every flight was canceled and every hotel room was booked). The goal is to capture some sense of the other person's experience to the maximum extent possible.

Deep acting brings greater rewards by generating a feedback loop of empathy from patients. Caregivers who are able to generate a virtuous cycle of empathy are more likely to feel compassion satisfaction. They are nourished by their work rather than exhausted by it.

Comparing empathy to acting may seem cynical. Moreover, the suggestion that clinicians should strive for superficial acting first and work toward deep acting is an ambitious goal that may not be achievable with every patient. My actor friends would say that skeptics don't fully grasp the nature of acting; it is not the same thing as pretending.

But the true major message I took home from this paper was that empathy is work. It takes energy and motivation to focus on every patient, to understand every patient's needs, and to convey that understanding. Clinicians need the training to deliver empathic care, but they also need support so that they can muster the energy and the motivation to deliver it not just when they feel like it but for every patient.

Ten Tactics for Acquiring Empathy

Acting isn't the only way to acquire empathy; a number of other approaches have been developed by psychologists, counselors, and educators. In his book, Hojat describes a fairly comprehensive set of 10 tactics that are specific to healthcare, all of which are consistent with the goal of understanding patients' concerns and experiences. Here are brief summaries of and comments on his 10 approaches:

1. **Improving interpersonal skills**

   Training programs can help clinicians improve their ability to recognize patients' negative emotions, concerns, and inner experiences so that they can explore those issues with the patient.[5] The key skills correspond to Hojat's focus on cognition, understanding, and communicating. Training gives caregivers practice in recognizing when patients are offering an opportunity for an empathic interaction by expressing emotions or worries. The caregiver can then respond empathetically, explore the issues, and convey understanding.

   A key focus of such training is recognizing the windows of opportunity in conversations with patients and not letting them pass. Developing more subtle skills such as nodding to give patients the sense that they are understood and giving appropriate verbal cues ("I see what you are worried about") is also highlighted. The importance of nonverbal communication such as tone of voice, touching, physical distance, and body posture (sitting at the same level as the patient, keeping the arms uncrossed) is stressed. Some programs even instruct clinicians to mirror patients' postures, gestures, breathing rates, and speech patterns.

   Several studies have shown that such training can lead to more empathic relationships and better patient experience, but exactly how it achieves these improvements remains something of a mystery. Is the benefit a result of the impact of individual acts such as touching the patient's arm? Or does the improvement result from conveying a general message: "I understand you, and it's my job to make things better for you"? The answer is probably somewhere in between.

2. **Audio recording, videotaping, or actual observation of encounters with patients**

Researchers studying empathy have long used audio recording and videotaping of encounters between clinicians and patients. An increasing number of healthcare delivery organizations are doing the same thing or having trained observers sit in on clinician-patient interactions. Of course, when clinicians know that they are being observed, they behave differently. What is surprising is that even when under observation, so many clinicians show a great deal of room for improvement.

In one study,[6] oncologists either missed or prematurely terminated conversations about patients' concerns 73 percent of the time. Other findings show similarly low rates of detecting or seizing opportunities for conveying empathy. How low? Let's just say that if baseball players had a similar batting average, they'd have a poor chance of making it to the major leagues. Physicians seem to be connecting emotionally with patients less reliably than baseball players are connecting a bat with a small, round, fast-moving sphere.

Data show that recorded or live observation can lead to improvement. Organizations that have used these approaches are convinced that many—but not all—clinicians sustain that improvement.

3. **Exposure to role models**

Role models are often discussed in the context of physicians at academic medical centers, but in fact they exist in all settings, among all types of clinicians and other medical personnel, and at every level of the healthcare system. Many (not all) of these role models demonstrate empathic skills as a core feature of their skill sets, but those role models are not systematically identified, and the nature of their skills is not widely shared. The pace of modern medicine and the number of clinicians involved in care at many medical centers work against identifying role models and developing their best practices into social norms.

4. **Role playing**

The Aging Game is an example of how role playing can enhance clinicians' ability to empathize. It was developed in 1989 to help medical students prepare to provide empathic care to the elderly.[7] The game has three stages. In the first, students are told to imagine that they are elderly and use earplugs to simulate hearing loss. In the second, students make a transition from independent living in one area to semidependent living in another and then transition to dependent living in which they are confined to wheelchairs and stretchers. The third stage of the game is a group discussion of the participants' experiences.

There are a variety of other forms of structured role playing in which devices such as goggles with film over the lenses simulate cataracts or heavy stockings simulate leg edema. Studies consistently show that students who go through such programs become more sensitive to patients' concerns.

5. **Shadowing a patient**

Many medical curricula routinely include shadowing of patients over prolonged periods. Such experiences help trainees understand that patients are not just an admission or a case but are human beings who are undergoing something important, often life-changing. An extreme—and extremely effective—version of patient shadowing is the longitudinal experience model for medical students pioneered at Cambridge Health Alliance in Massachusetts.

In this model, medical students do not rotate through traditional blocks of time defined by specialties (e.g., surgery, pediatrics, obstetrics, and gynecology). Instead, they follow a large group of patients through every type of care: primary care, hospitalizations, nursing homes, and care at home. The focus is on what patients need rather than what doctors do. The assumption is that students will learn what doctors do as they help meet their patients' needs.

When students who went through this track were compared with students who had traditional training, the longitudinal approach was associated with better academic performance on standardized tests as well as greater satisfaction and idealism. These data are based on a small number of students, of course, and research to evaluate this concept on a broader scale is under way. However, the results offer hope that more exposure to patients over time can lead to greater empathy rather than greater burnout for clinicians.

6. **Hospitalization and illness experiences**

When clinicians or trainees pretend to be patients, that is, persons being admitted to the hospital, they increase their insight into what patients are going through. Some organizations have personnel go through such exercises with or without the knowledge of the caregivers.

A variant on this theme is to disseminate commentary from clinicians and other colleagues who themselves have become ill. For obvious reasons, their comments resonate with their colleagues in a way that the same words from a patient might not.

7. **Studying of literature and the arts**

    Many medical schools and healthcare delivery organizations promote appreciation of the arts—novels, nonfiction literature, plays, films, paintings, photography, and the like—as an approach to deepening appreciation for and insight into the perspectives of other human beings. Several studies have shown that such programs (e.g., intensive reading of Tolstoy's *The Death of Ivan Ilyich*) can enhance students' empathy. Whether such programs lead to durable increases in empathy and whether they appeal only to clinicians who already have strong empathic skills is uncertain. Nevertheless, they clearly seem to enrich the lives of both teachers and students.

8. **Improving narrative skills**

    Everyone listens more attentively to a story than to a recitation of facts. Accordingly, one approach to enhancing empathy skills entails getting clinicians to understand patients' experiences as stories as opposed to simply collecting clinical data. As one of my clinical mentors would say, "Don't just tell me a patient's age, race, and gender. Tell me about him. Don't say a seventy-six-year-old white male. Tell me he is a seventy-six-year-old former piano teacher so I can begin to understand what it means for him to lose his ability to use his left arm."

    To think in terms of stories, it is critical to listen for them and then write or tell them. Patients can tell when clinicians are listening to them in this way. Conversely, patients can tell when clinicians are not attentive to the overall arc of their stories. Some programs train clinicians and students in "narrative competence" through reflective reading, writing, and discussions.

9. **Theatrical performances**

Beyond reading, writing, and telling stories is portraying them. Dramatic performances by real or simulated patients have been memorable interventions in many medical communities. By observing or acting in plays that capture the experiences of patients with serious conditions (e.g., AIDS and cancer), clinicians can enhance their readiness to understand patients' issues in real life.

10. **The Balint method**

The Balint training program was developed by the Hungarian psychoanalyst Michael Balint at the Tavistock Institute in London. It is based on the assumption that many clinicians have spent so much time training for their medical work that they may not have had an opportunity to develop skills in the interpersonal aspects of patient care. In regular small group meetings over one to three years, clinicians discuss behavioral and emotional issues related to interactions with their patients. The groups are often moderated by a psychoanalyst or another mental health professional.

The Empathy Short Course

Learning the basics of empathy doesn't require a huge investment of time. Helen Riess and her colleagues at Massachusetts General Hospital have demonstrated that a month of training can increase physicians' empathy enough to get them significantly higher ratings by patients.[8] She recruited 99 residents and fellows in six specialties—anesthesiology, internal medicine, orthopedics, ophthalmology, psychiatry, and surgery—more than half of whom reported that they had less empathy for patients than they did when they began their residencies.

Riess and colleagues randomized the trainees into two groups. One group participated in three hourlong sessions of empathy and relationship training spread over four weeks; the other group continued with standard medical training. Not surprisingly, by the end of the study, the intervention group had a better understanding of the neurobiology of empathy and an improved ability to decode subtle facial expressions.

However, what mattered more was what their patients experienced. At the beginning and end of the study, the patients rated their doctors by the Consultation and Relational Empathy (CARE) Measure,[9] a 10-item survey in which patients used a 5-point scale to evaluate their doctors' demeanor on their last visit. At the end of the study, the control group had lost ground, with their patients scoring them an average of 1.5 points lower on the CARE scale than they had at the beginning. In contrast, the intervention group had gained an average of 0.7 point.

What Does Empathy Look Like?

The challenging reality is that empathic care is not a simple, straightforward action that clinicians can perform as reliably as washing their hands. It cannot be boiled down to a checklist of behaviors or an etiquette manual.

Empathic care is something that happens between clinicians and patients and often with patients' families as well. If it is more like dancing than running for clinicians, it is dancing with new partners every 15 minutes. Patients and clinicians vary in their temperaments, and the fact is that we all vary as individuals from day to day and even from hour to hour. The result is that empathic care can seem like snowflakes: when you look at relationships between clinicians and patients, no two are exactly the same.

When I talk to doctors and patients about their relationships, I am often startled at the descriptions of their interactions. "My doctor has empathy in spades," one woman said. We'll call her Gloria. She was referring to her primary care doctor, an internist who is well known among her colleagues for her directness, which sometimes comes off as bluntness. We'll call her Dr. Smith. Here is the example Gloria provided:

"Several years ago, Dr. Smith found what seemed to be a large fibroid during my annual pelvic exam. She didn't seem too concerned but suggested I have an ultrasound. I had the test on a Friday morning a few weeks later and left that afternoon for a long weekend in New York. When I came home the following Tuesday, there was a voice mail from Dr. Smith's office asking me to come in that afternoon. I knew immediately that the ultrasound had found something serious.

"When I got to her office I expected the usual 15-minute wait, but Dr. Smith was at the reception desk to meet me. 'When I saw your ultrasound results, I almost threw up,' she said as soon as we were alone. 'It's ovarian.'"

"And that was empathy?" I asked.

"Exactly," Gloria said. "Because I felt like I was going to vomit, too."

I have never told a patient that one of his or her lab tests made me want to throw up. Indeed, reserved as I am, the very idea of saying that unsettles me. But somehow Dr. Smith sensed that this was just the thing to say to Gloria at that moment. Gloria *loved* Dr. Smith for saying it; she took that comment to mean that Dr. Smith completely understood what she was feeling and was going to be on and at her side every step of the difficult path ahead.

Blunt though she can be, Dr. Smith knows what empathy is: understanding what another person is feeling and conveying that understanding. Dr. Smith's reciprocal expression of nausea was a visceral statement that she understood what Gloria was feeling. Dr. Smith also sensed how this particular patient wanted to be treated. She knew that Gloria would rather be given a direct bolus of bad news than have it spoon-fed to her in bits and pieces.

Dr. Smith has a large and diverse practice. I can't imagine that all her patients would like hearing that their test results made her sick to her stomach. What do Dr. Smith's other patients think of her? In fact, her ratings are superb, pretty much the equivalent of perfect SAT scores. Perhaps she attracts patients who all want care of a certain style, but it is more likely that she knows how to deliver empathic care differently for different patients.

Dr. Smith is constantly adjusting what she does for and says to her patients. What stays the same is her reliability in making the effort to tune in to the needs of the person in front of her. It's work—draining work, in fact—to do that. It's art as well. And when it goes well, it is part of what makes medicine such a fabulous field in which to work.

Barriers to Empathy

Empathy is innate, but it can also be learned. However, certain circumstances can make it difficult to learn how to be empathic or to maintain empathy.

History abounds with examples of what happens on a large scale in the absence of empathy, the most extreme of which include genocide, slavery, terrorism, and economic exploitation. The concept of moral disengagement describes how people might focus on something good that they are doing and wall themselves off from considering the negative impact on others who are outside their self-imposed field of vision. The result can be extreme empathy within a group but the opposite for everyone else.

Yet these periods of moral disengagement—though dramatic—are sporadic episodes in history. There is a societal advantage to sustaining empathy, as suggested by the political scientist Robert Axelrod.[10] Axelrod is a game theory expert who was well aware of how logic suggests that human beings are selfish and how they do what it takes to survive, with the net result often being a failure to cooperate in ways that would have enhanced the fortunes of all. However, Axelrod was struck by the fact that society does not devolve into chaos, or at least not as often as it might. Instead, people find a way to cooperate, often at the most unexpected moments.

One of those moments was in the winter of 1914 in the trenches of the Western front during World War I. This was the scene of the famous Christmas Eve soccer game between British and German forces, but as Axelrod described it, the actual extent of the cooperation was much greater. Once the two armies realized that they were stuck together and that neither was likely to be victorious any time soon, they developed cooperative behaviors in which injuries were minimized on both sides. German snipers would demonstrate their prowess by firing at the walls of cottages in a tight target area until they had cut a hole in a wall, but they would not fire at British soldiers. That encouraged and rewarded British soldiers for also doing what they could to avoid harming the Germans. Artillery from both sides deliberately overshot their targets.

This live-and-let-live approach was obviously not the major story of World War I, and commanding officers behind the front lines tried to eliminate it whenever possible. But the lesson that emerges from these and other examples of the evolution of cooperation is that when two parties are brought face-to-face and become invested in a future that they will be sharing, the ability to understand the needs of the other side naturally emerges.

With this insight, it becomes obvious why so many wars begin with the effort to dehumanize the other side and eliminate empathy for the enemy. The implication for healthcare is that anything that dehumanizes patients also destroys our ability to meet their need for empathic care.

Distraction: The Enemy of Empathy

Patients want empathy and clinicians see themselves as empathic, so what's the problem? One primary care physician at Cambridge Health Alliance, an articulate young woman, summarized it for me this way:

"I want to be empathic, I really do. But it is so hard to focus on anyone or anything these days," she said. "I try to listen. I try to look at them. But in the back of my mind, I am aware of e-mails arriving in my in-box. I hear little pings and feel little vibrations. I'm aware of the three patients who are waiting because I'm running late, and the telephone calls I have to answer, and the worrisome lab results I have to run to the ground. That's not to mention the issues from my life at home that also need to be addressed by five o'clock today, and the reality is that I don't have any time before seven o'clock."

Distractions are the destroyers of focus. Such distractions seem almost inherent to modern life, but arguably, they pose bigger problems in healthcare than they do anywhere else. It's one thing for people to cast glances at their smartphones at the dinner table or during other types of business interactions, but if patients realize that a physician is not taking in what they are saying because the physician's mind is somewhere else, they're not going to feel that they are getting good healthcare.

The need to focus the attention of busy, hardworking clinicians on patients is a major reason why I changed my thinking about the use of the word *suffering* in the spring of 2013. I used to think that invoking suffering to describe what patients were experiencing was sensational and manipulative. I still think that is true, but I believe that this kind of manipulation is just what we need to overcome the distractions of modern life so that doctors and nurses can concentrate on the patients in front of them, an essential first step in the delivery of care with real empathy.

I described this modest epiphany on the road to empathy in an article titled "The Word That Shall Not Be Spoken"[11] that was published in 2013 in the *New England Journal of Medicine*, where I was then a part-time associate editor. Although I was a primary care physician and cardiologist at Brigham and Women's Hospital, my main job at that time was as network president of Partners HealthCare System, the integrated delivery system started by the Brigham and Massachusetts General Hospital in 1994. In that role, I worked with my colleagues to improve the quality and efficiency of care in our hospitals and across the continuum of care. As we did that work, we would often discuss patients' experiences in our delivery system, which stretched across eastern Massachusetts. We worked to reduce their confusion (and that of their clinicians) as they navigated our complex organizations.

We knew that anxiety was inevitable for some patients because of the severity of their medical problems. But we also knew that there was unnecessary anxiety that had nothing to do with their diseases or treatments: the waiting time, the uncertainty about what was going to happen next, the worries that their clinicians were not quite in sync with one another. We worked to reduce that anxiety. It made good business sense, and it was obviously the right thing to do.

As proud as I was (and remain) of that work, I was taken aback when I met Pat Ryan in March 2013. He had recently assumed the role of CEO of Press Ganey, and after talking to people inside the organization and its clients, he had decided that his company should do more than collect data. He thought the goal should be to reduce the suffering of patients: suffering from disease, suffering from treatment, and suffering from the dysfunction of the delivery system.

My first reaction, which I said out loud at our breakfast, was that he was interested in the same things as my colleagues and I. My second reaction, which I kept to myself, was that the word *suffering* would take some getting used to. I didn't doubt that my patients were suffering in a wide variety of ways, but like many clinicians, I had a hard time receiving feedback that our care was less than perfect.

I was certainly uncomfortable with the notion that our coordination issues might actually be inflicting misery on patients. Nevertheless, it was hard to object to the use of the word *suffering*. Therefore, I just said what was true: I couldn't remember the last time we had used the word *suffering* when discussing improvements in any organization, including my own.

Later, when I discussed the conversation with physician colleagues, they also had a negative reaction to the word *suffering* even though we agreed that suffering was exactly what so many patients were experiencing. When we analyzed what made us uncomfortable, one conclusion was that the term was too vague.

"I want to be told about things relevant to doctors, things that I personally can do something about," one physician said. "Like anxiety. There is a diagnostic code for visits for anxiety. I can prescribe pills for anxiety. I can bill for visits for anxiety. But suffering is too amorphous for me to know what to do." Aware of the irony, he said that too much talk about patients' suffering might distract clinicians from doing what they could to relieve its specific causes.

Another colleague raised a darker theme. "The problem with the word *suffering* is that it makes you feel bad," he said. "I know my patients are suffering and that I do things differently for the patients who are closest to me. I don't let them wait. I don't let them be confused about what is happening. I make sure that their various specialists are talking to each other, and I make sure the patient knows when those conversations have occurred. But it's a bottomless pit. If I tried to do everything I could to relieve every patient's suffering, I'd never get home at night."

We all understood. He was bringing up a type of disparity in healthcare different from the ones we had previously discussed. There is plenty of information about gaps in quality of care received by the poor compared with the rich and differences in the outcomes of care among racial groups. His comment suggested that there might be another type of disparity hidden within the health-care system: between the patients with whom clinicians readily empathize and everyone else.

The implications were painful, even ugly. None of us see ourselves as people who would stand by while someone is suffering. None of us want to lead or be part of organizations that willfully ignore suffering, let alone inflict suffering by being oblivious to patients' worries. But we know that for some patients we make the extra phone calls, have the extra meetings, and do whatever we can to reduce the chaos of the system. We base our perceptions of ourselves on how we take care of those patients, but we know we don't do the same or believe we cannot do the same for everyone else.

It was hard to avoid the conclusion that we clinicians avoid the word *suffering* even though we know it is real for our patients because if we admit that it exists, we have to take responsibility for it. The idea of taking responsibility for reducing suffering is overwhelming for us as individuals, and we already feel overwhelmed by our duties and obligations.

I felt both better and worse when I learned that my colleagues and I were not the only ones who avoided that word. Most academic medical journals use the *AMA Manual of Style*, which says, "Avoid describing persons as victims or with other emotional terms that suggest helplessness (afflicted with, suffering from, stricken with, maimed)."[12] In implementing this guideline, journals tend to allow *programs* to "suffer" in print for reasons such as lack of funding or leadership. But *patients* are not allowed to suffer from diseases or complications; copy editors are trained at many journals to change "The patient suffered from complications . . ." to "The patient experienced complications. . . ."

I felt better because it was good to know that my colleagues and I were not callous outliers. I felt worse because I suspected that clinicians were avoiding the word *suffering* because it compels a response that we are not sure we can deliver. That made me wonder if using that word to describe what patients experience might be the first step toward more empathic care.

It was around that time that I learned that the word *patient* comes from the Latin word *patiens*, which is derived from the verb *patior*, which means "I am suffering." Suddenly the term *patient-centered care* took on a new meaning. It was about the detection and reduction of suffering, and those acts put empathy at the core of what medicine is about. I was optimistic that my colleagues could and would rise to the challenge once it was fully understood.

How Empathy Can Be Eroded

Some researchers have speculated that empathy may be similar to language in that it is readily acquired in infancy and can continue to grow throughout life. However, like language, empathy can wither if it isn't practiced regularly or if it is not prized. (Think of all the immigrant children who have been encouraged to shed their native tongues so that they can be accepted more rapidly into their adopted country.)

A few sociologists have argued that empathy implies a sense that we're all in this together. They maintain that empathy was not valued in the climate of the 1970s and 1980s: the Me Decade and the Greed Is Good Decade. In that period, individualism and personal accomplishment at almost any price reigned supreme.

Coincidentally or otherwise, those two decades were also the beginning of an era of incredible technological advances in medicine. Cardiology expanded exponentially as cardiac catheterization and open-heart surgery were becoming commonplace; chemotherapy was transforming oncology; and computed tomography (CT), positron emission tomography (PET), and MRI made radiology a technologically thrilling field. Bench scientists were revealing the basic mechanisms of atherosclerosis, inflammation, and devastating hereditary conditions such as familial hypercholesterolemia, cystic fibrosis, and Huntington's disease. Rapid-fire advances in biochemistry and molecular biology were enabling rational drug design and the debut of blockbuster drugs.

In this climate, medical school and training were not led by—or for—the gentle-hearted. Medicine was growing increasingly difficult and competitive. One colleague told me how one of his professors used to stop him in the hallway and say, "How much did you sleep last night?" Regardless of what he answered, the professor's response was "That's too much."

During clinical rounds, the emphasis was on acquiring diagnostic and procedural skills, not a compassionate bedside manner. Medical students tended to focus on getting into the best residency program for their specialty and ultimately becoming affiliated with a prestigious medical organization. Under extreme pressure, constantly sleep-deprived, and occasionally feeling abused by senior staff, physicians in training tended to put most of their energy into staying on their personal courses.

Several studies have shown that empathy declines during medical training. One cited reason is that trainees distance themselves from patients to protect themselves from psychological damage. Another is that the demands of training don't leave them with the time or emotional energy to empathize with patients.

In one study, internal medicine residents at the University of Pennsylvania completed the Interpersonal Reactivity Index (IRI) and Profile of Mood States (POMS) at six points during their residency training. The former evaluated empathy; the latter, resilience. The researchers found that the residents were in relatively good shape at the beginning of the program. In fact, their scores indicated that they were more empathic, vigorous, and emotionally stable than the general population of graduate students. However, their mood scores plummeted rapidly, reaching a nadir midway through their internship. Although their depression and anger abated over time, returning to baseline by the end of their residencies, their vigor and empathy remained low.[13]

These are generalizations, of course, and trainees vary in their experiences and responses. Much depends on the role models around them. During my training, I had a fabulous faculty preceptor, Phyllis Jen, who was the first physician I had met who contacted every patient with laboratory results regardless of whether they were normal or abnormal. Today this follow-up is an expected practice, but in the early 1980s it was unusual. Even today some physicians do not communicate with patients about normal results.

But Phyllis saw it differently. "I figure that if I stick a needle into someone's arm and suck blood out of them, I kind of owe it to them to let them know the results," she said with a shrug. "I know I would want that."

She was putting herself in the patients' place, understanding what they needed, and giving it to them. Phyllis did not make the other physicians and trainees in her practice communicate with patients after every lab test, but she set an example in this and many other ways. By doing so, she set standards that trainees like myself did not want to fail to meet. (Phyllis Jen died in 2009, and the primary care center where I practice is named in her honor.)

If doctors are low on empathy at the beginning of their careers, the current medical climate doesn't reliably encourage it to bloom again. In a 2005 paper, Sharyn Potter and John McKinlay discussed the degradation of the physician-patient relationship during the twentieth century.[14] At the beginning of that period, it was a paternalistic relationship in which doctors' superior knowledge gave them all the power. Patients didn't seem to mind the inequality; they had a high level of trust in their doctors.

In that era, the physician and the patient were often members of the same community (at least in communities that were sufficiently well-to-do to have physicians living in them). The relationships between doctors and patients had both longitude and latitude. Physicians had known many of their adult patients since infancy and might have even delivered them. They also knew their families and friends. They ran into them at community events and were aware of their successes and reversals.

If empathy implies appreciating where someone is coming from, midcentury physicians didn't have to work hard to gain it. They knew in advance how much urging patients would need to stop smoking or lose weight, how much discomfort they were willing to tolerate, whether they were likely to comply with a complicated regimen, and exactly who their caretakers would be if they became disabled.

In many ways, the relationship Gloria has with Dr. Smith is a throwback to the last century. Dr. Smith has been in practice at a major Boston teaching hospital for decades, since the very beginning of her career. Gloria has been her patient for 20 years, and she's not unique in that respect. Dr. Smith values her longitudinal relationships with her patients. She knows not only their medical histories but also their life stories: what's going on with their careers and how their kids are doing. She visits her patients in the hospital even when she's not the admitting physician and makes house calls to dying patients.

But a variety of forces make Dr. Smith feel like she is swimming against the tide as she tries to preserve empathic longitudinal relationships. Medical progress means many more clinicians are involved in the care even of patients with routine medical problems. It often seems that physicians have to give so much energy to keeping their colleagues up to date through the electronic medical record that there is little time for actually looking at or listening to the patient.

Today few physicians can expect to have the kind of longitudinal relationship with their patients that Dr. Smith has with Gloria. Only a third of physicians deliver primary care. The specialties of internal medicine, family medicine, pediatrics, and geriatrics have shrunk as their relative incomes have declined. An increasing number of physicians are in households in which both adults work in demanding jobs, and so neither partner can work endless hours. After all, someone has to get home to help the children with their homework or walk the dog. That means patients are "cross-covered" and often seen by someone who does not know them well in their hour of need.

Recognizing the Lack of Empathy

An important step in stemming the erosion of empathy and cultivating its reemergence is to recognize when it has been lost. *Compassion fatigue* is a term coined in the late 1980s as a synonym for secondary traumatic stress syndrome. It describes the effects of taking care of people who are enduring traumatic events. Caregivers with compassion fatigue may feel angry or helpless and often turn off their own emotions as a defense mechanism. Compassion fatigue is particularly prevalent in specialists who treat the groups of patients in the greatest distress: psychiatrists, emergency physicians, and palliative care specialists.

A painful irony of compassion fatigue is that the people who have the most empathy are the most likely to lose it. Charles Figley, a pioneer in the study of compassion fatigue, has shown that exposure to patients' pain and suffering elicits empathy from doctors and nurses but that sustaining empathy over time taxes the emotional energy of caregivers. The risk of compassion fatigue increases with continued exposure to suffering, especially if it is compounded by other job stresses, such as increases in patient load or personal issues.

Compassion fatigue can be measured with a variety of tools, including the widely used ProQOL (Professional Quality of Life) questionnaire. For example, in one study of emergency doctors and nurses in the United Kingdom's National Health Service, the ProQOL tool was used to identify emergency medicine doctors and nurses who were "compassion satisfied" or "compassion fatigued." Clinicians in the fatigued group were more likely to report that they were often irritable when dealing with patients or colleagues. They also felt that they weren't able to deliver as high a standard of care as they once had. More than half said they wanted to retire early.

When interviewed, clinicians with compassion fatigue described a sense of emotional and physical depletion from having to work longer shifts during high-volume periods and returning to the regular schedule with no break after having been on call. Many also felt unsupported by others on their team.

For example, one clinician said, "The elements that I have control over are outweighed by the magnitude of the effects of other people's decisions that are impacting negatively on the service . . . when the combination of that lack of control and personal exhaustion comes in, you start getting demoralized . . . you can't be that calm relaxed person you want to be for your staff and for your patients."

In contrast, the "compassion satisfied" group reported having developed strategies to deal with the intensity of their work, such as exercising and taking a short break when they found their patience fraying. They felt good about their teammates, describing the support of colleagues and team spirit as important in preventing burnout. They also tended to have greater variety in their jobs and the opportunity to shift from clinical care to administrative work, which functioned as a pressure-release valve.

One of the salient differences between the two groups was in the empathy they felt toward their patients. In one question, the interviewers asked them to describe how they reacted to people who sought emergency care for nonurgent problems. Those in the satisfied group seemed to share a philosophy that all were entitled to care regardless of the severity of their illness, whereas those in the fatigued group were more likely to view such patients as less worthy of compassion—especially if they were demanding or complaining—because they didn't belong in an emergency facility.[15]

Empathy as Essential to Excellence

When care is not empathic and clinicians realize it, they have a common response: they cringe. That is not the way they want to see themselves. But when clinicians think of quality, they tend to focus on technical issues ("Do we have the latest equipment?") or their reliability in complying with evidence-based guidelines. In fact, as individuals and as teams, clinicians have much more reliability in delivering evidence-based care than in delivering empathetic care even though compassion is at the core of their self-images.

The irony is that clinicians tend to take for granted that care is going to be compassionate, whereas patients take for granted that care is going to be technically excellent. Both are important, of course, but it is risky to assume that either will naturally occur if good people just work hard. They both take disciplined management, and improvement on one does not guarantee improvement on the other. The healthcare organizations that rank highest for clinical care in the annual surveys conducted by *U.S. News & World Report* don't always get comparable scores in patient satisfaction surveys.

Cleveland Clinic provides a great case in point. In 2008, the first year Hospital Consumer Assessment of Healthcare Providers and Systems (HCAHPS) results were publicly released, the hospital, which was fourth in the *U.S. News* rankings, was barely in the top half of hospitals in patient satisfaction. Only 72 percent of Cleveland Clinic doctors and 62 percent of nurses scored high in the ability to communicate.

The HCAHPS data came as a wake-up call to Toby Cosgrove, the CEO of Cleveland Clinic. As James Merlino recounts in

Service Fanatics, Cosgrove set out to improve the patient experience at every turn. He appointed Merlino as chief experience officer (CXO), and they decided that the foundation of the makeover should be to inject empathy into every facet of the patient experience, just as service at every point in a customer's stay is the key to the success of world-class hotels such as the Ritz-Carlton. To communicate the idea that the staff and the patients were part of a single organism, they instituted regular training in emotional intelligence for their 2,200 managers.

Merlino also commissioned a video, *Empathy: The Human Connection to Patient Care,* to underscore the human commonalities of hospital staff and patients. The video, which has no dialogue, follows several people as they walk through the hospital, with only brief captions to indicate what they are experiencing. A patient tethered to IVs and tubes is identified as "10,000 miles from home," and an ICU physician as "ending a 12-hour shift." In one particularly moving sequence, a young girl pets a therapy dog; her caption reads "Visiting dad for the last time." The video ends with the words "If you could stand in someone's shoes. See what they see. Feel what they feel. Would you treat them differently?" The video, which was intended for internal use, went viral on YouTube, garnering more than 2 million views.

The message that the leadership at Cleveland Clinic sent to their colleagues is increasingly widespread. Technical excellence is not enough. Safety is not enough. Efficiency is not enough. Clinicians have to be reliable in every way, including delivery of care that is empathic. Excellence means consistency in delivering care the way it should be—for every patient every time.

What's the path to empathic care? Acting and short courses in empathy can provide a jump-start, but empathy deepens with practice. As Larson and Yao (see note 4) put it, "Empathy, considered by many an art, cannot be achieved simply through explicit teaching and mimicking.... This is a slow immersion process that can be

likened to the maturing of a fine wine."Transforming an organization from a technocracy to one powered by empathy won't happen
overnight. To drive that change and sustain improvement, the next
key step to master is measurement.

CHAPTER

4 | Measurement

We have the will, but we only partially understand the way. We know the problem: the chaos of modern medicine and the destructive impact it can have on coordination and empathy. We understand the strategic imperative to improve patient-centered care, and we have pretty clear ideas about what we need to do: deliver compassionate, coordinated care. However, our knowledge of the science to support these critical steps—what to measure to assess our progress, how to collect the data, how to analyze them, and how to use them to create change—is far from perfect and often is a subject of controversy.

To drive improvement—*sustained* improvement—we need measures, we need data, and we need wisdom about how to use them. Measures and data give providers insight into how they are doing compared with others and where opportunities to improve may exist. The real goal is not to rank providers on their empathy but to help them improve. Organizations want them to deliver their best possible care to the next patient they see, and the patient after that, and the patient after that. Performance improvement is really about changing the future, but it requires honest and rigorous assessment of the present and the past.

This is where many efforts to improve empathy in care have stalled. If healthcare is to be organized around meeting patients' needs, it seems obvious that patients must be the ultimate judges of providers' success. However, providers traditionally have had deep reservations about whether data from patients can be used to judge the quality of healthcare. This chapter will review and address the most common reservations and describe the rapid evolution and state of the science for the collection and use of data. First, to provide the context for the current and likely future states, we need to understand where we have come from.

A Brief History of Patient Experience Measurement

The field of patient experience measurement is burgeoning, but it is a relatively new business function, and when the field first developed, its goals were different from what they are today.

Patient satisfaction became a topic of interest to hospitals in the 1980s, which, although just a few decades ago, was a qualitatively different era in healthcare. In fact, throughout most of the twentieth century the conventional wisdom held that our healthcare was generally excellent—and beyond measurement. In the years leading up to the millennium, there had been so much medical progress that there was some uncertainty about whether new tests and treatments were being used wisely, and guidelines had been developed to try to prevent overuse and underuse. The preservation of physicians' autonomy to do what they judged best for patients was often invoked as the first principle of high-quality healthcare.

As was noted in Chapter 2, the publication of two groundbreaking Institute of Medicine (IOM) reports—*To Err Is Human* in 2000 and *Crossing the Quality Chasm* in 2001—revealed deficits in safety, reliability, and patients' overall experience. This did not come as a complete surprise to healthcare providers, of course. There had been growing concern that healthcare might not be as safe as many assumed, and researchers had begun to collect data on how often patients were injured by their care. The series of studies in New York State and elsewhere by Troyen Brennan and his Harvard colleagues showed that potentially preventable injuries were surprisingly common and that they had little relationship to the medical malpractice system.[1] This research ultimately created the context for the first IOM report, with its vivid image of a 747 crashing every day to capture the toll of medical injuries on patients in the United States. Although that image was considered sensational by many, it was effective in driving change and helped create the patient safety movement in healthcare.

Patient safety was not the only dimension of quality that was recognized as problematic. *Crossing the Quality Chasm* also highlighted five other aims: care should be effective, patient-centered, timely, efficient, and equitable. In its recommendations, the IOM defined goals, including the following:

- That healthcare should be responsive to patients' needs at all times (24 hours a day every day)

- That the care system should be designed to meet the most common types of needs but flexible enough to accommodate the needs and values of individuals

- That patients be the source of control and have the necessary information and the opportunity to exercise as much control as they wanted over healthcare decisions that affect them

- That clinicians and patients communicate effectively and share information

- That the health system anticipate patients' needs, not just respond to events

- That clinicians and organizations cooperate, communicate, and coordinate their efforts

These goals are at the core of strategy for most healthcare organizations today, but they were not on the radar of many hospitals and other provider organizations in the 1980s, when the management of these organizations first started talking about patient satisfaction. At that time, hospital leaders were interested in addressing and preventing patient complaints and were seeking ways to improve "service" as a way of competing for market share. Since hospital leaders assumed that the actual clinical care they were providing was excellent—or at least just fine—they believed that they needed to differentiate themselves by providing "wow experiences" such as beautiful settings, smiling and friendly personnel, excellent food, musicians in the lobby, artwork on the walls, and easy parking. Doctors and nurses weren't opposed to those efforts but did not think they were critical to actual patient care and mustered only modest enthusiasm. Clinicians felt, "This is what administrators do, not what we do."

This orientation toward "hotel functions" was not a reflection of naiveté on the part of healthcare providers. As was described in Chapter 2, in that era patients could generally go to any provider they chose without any difference in their personal costs. Hospitals could thrive if they got patients in the door, into their beds, and into their procedure rooms. With enough market share, hospitals would be indispensable to health insurance companies and could negotiate "cost-plus" contracts that covered their expenses for all their populations—including the uninsured or underinsured—and still provide a financial margin. Thus, the focus for hospital leaders was improving their brand.

Today, the driver of the healthcare marketplace is becoming competition on value: meeting patients' needs as efficiently as possible. To improve value, organizations need to measure and make progress on the types of issues that were the focus of *Crossing the Quality Chasm*. But when the patient satisfaction business emerged in the 1980s, it was oriented toward brand, not value. Indeed, *patient satisfaction* was the prevailing term used for measuring patient views of care because it reflected the notion of the patient as a consumer who must be satisfied to be retained.

Irwin Press, PhD, a Notre Dame professor who taught a course on medical anthropology, took time during the early 1980s to observe the complexities of patient care in the multicultural environment of the University of Miami's Jackson Memorial Hospital. His original research focused on the experience of individuals whose cultural beliefs about health and wellness differed from those of Western medicine. He quickly realized, however, that medical treatment felt foreign to pretty much everyone, not just to non-Westerners. Most patients, whatever their cultural backgrounds, felt that they were on unfamiliar turf when they found themselves in a land of experts who had their own procedures, language, and social mores.

Toward the end of his stay at Jackson Memorial, Press mentioned to an administrator that if patients were more satisfied with their experience of care, they might be less likely to sue the hospital for real or imagined errors. That notion was enticing to the administrator, who let Press review malpractice claims against the hospital. Press found what Brennan and his colleagues would later document in New York State: an enormous proportion of claims had little or nothing to do with problems in technical quality. What seemed to be driving many of the legal actions was the fact that patients and their families had become angry and upset.

As Press spoke about his observations, the idea that patients might be less likely to sue doctors and hospitals if they were more satisfied with their care caught the attention of healthcare managers nationally. The number and cost of suits were rising, creating the sense of a malpractice crisis. In addition, healthcare was beginning to feel the early impact of cost pressures, and managed care insurance plans were starting to steer patients toward some hospitals and away from others. Fearful of losing market share, hospitals sought expertise from other business sectors, including service industries such as resorts, hotels, and amusement parks.

In this context, the patient satisfaction business was born, with the two major drivers being concern about complaints that might turn into malpractice suits and fear of potential loss of market share. Press teamed with a Notre Dame colleague, Rod Ganey, PhD, an expert in statistics and survey methods, and in 1985 they founded Press Ganey, the company I joined in 2013. In addition to measuring patients' overall satisfaction and willingness to recommend an organization, the company measured the evaluation of care that patients received in terms of the clarity of communication, the efficiency of processes, the extent to which care was responsive and personalized, and the empathy of the care providers.

Press Ganey started measuring patient satisfaction with surveys mailed to samples of patients after their hospitalization. Growing interest in the results of patient satisfaction surveys attracted several other companies, including National Research Corporation (NRC), Gallup, HealthStream, Professional Research Consultants, Inc. (PRC), and Avatar, to the field. The Joint Commission, the leading accreditation agency for hospitals, added a requirement that hospitals measure patient satisfaction in some format to obtain accreditation. The settings of care for which data were sought expanded to include outpatient care, emergency departments, and ambulatory surgery, among others. Consulting companies started to offer advice on how to improve satisfaction.

In the wake of the IOM reports, the federal government became actively interested in patient experience. The Centers for Medicare & Medicaid Services (CMS) and the Agency for

Healthcare Research and Quality (AHRQ) worked with researchers to develop the Hospital Consumer Assessment of Healthcare Providers and Systems (HCAHPS) survey, a standardized instrument that is administered to randomly selected patients after discharge from the hospital. The HCAHPS survey was approved by the National Quality Forum in 2005 and implemented by CMS in 2006, and the first voluntary public reporting of HCAHPS results began in 2008.

HCAHPS went from being voluntary to being a fact of life for hospitals during the next few years. Hospitals received a financial incentive for participating in HCAHPS ("pay for reporting"), and eligible participation increased to nearly 95 percent. With the Affordable Care Act of 2010, portions of hospital Medicare reimbursement were tied to performance on HCAHPS, beginning with hospital discharges in 2012.

These same broad trends are playing out in other sectors of healthcare delivery. In sum, the trends are as follow:

- Standardized tools are being developed, tested, and then implemented with the suffix CAHPS (e.g., CG-CAHPS, or Clinician and Groups CAHPS, which is designed to drive improvement in care in doctors' offices).

- These tools are used on a voluntary basis at first, and then implementation is greatly enhanced through the use of financial incentives for reporting.

- Eventually, the tools become mandatory as financial incentives are tied to actual performance.

- As the tools are used, performance improves. Providers that stand still—that is, do nothing and have the same performance year after year—start to fall behind their competition (see Figure 4.1).

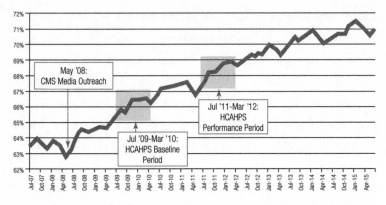

Figure 4.1   National HCAHPS "Rate This Hospital" average top box percentage trend since inception

Patient Satisfaction Versus Patient Experience

Another important change occurred in the years after the IOM reports: the term *patient satisfaction* began to give way to *patient experience*. This change seems a semantic nuance to many but is actually of historical significance. The IOM reports had revealed that there were important quality problems that needed to be addressed in healthcare. The challenges for clinicians and administrators amounted to something much more important than soothing ruffled feathers or attracting patients with wow experiences. There were basic issues related to providers' ability to meet patients' needs with reliability, efficiency, and safety that needed to be addressed.

Providers started to realize that patients do not come to hospitals or physician offices because they want to be pampered or have a recreational experience. Patients seek healthcare because they are worried, anxious, frightened, or in pain. They want relief from suffering, including prevention of anticipated suffering. As was described in Chapter 2, they want good clinicians who work well together and listen to patients' concerns. They want to be able to trust those clinicians. They want peace of mind that things are as good as they can be in light of the cards they have been dealt. They hope that their care will be safe, compassionate, and coordinated.

If patient satisfaction reflects whether the care conforms to patients' expectations, patient experience reflects everything that directly or indirectly affects patients across the continuum of care, including the expectations that patients bring to their healthcare encounters. *Everything* means every single thing: not just the care and the service that patients receive but also the relief of their suffering, physical discomfort, and anxiety. It is not defined completely by the responses to a series of yes-or-no questions about whether an important step such as receiving an explanation of test results occurred.

Think of patient satisfaction as an interim measure: "I am satisfied that what was supposed to happen with my care actually happened." Think of patient experience as the more critical outcome measure: "I have peace of mind that everyone worked well together to meet my needs as fully as possible." The latter is a deeper and more holistic measure, and it presents a tougher challenge: clinicians must be involved and engaged if there is to be improvement.

How does patient experience relate to other outcomes? Michael Porter's classic *New England Journal of Medicine* paper "What Is Value in Health Care?"[2] describes a three-tier hierarchy for measuring and thinking about patient outcomes. Porter points out that there is no single outcome that tells the full story for any group of patients; multiple outcomes collectively define success. The complexity of medicine means that multiple outcomes must be pursued, and sometimes competing outcomes must be weighed against each other (e.g., near-term safety versus long-term functionality).

In Porter's hierarchy, the most important outcomes are at the top, and lower-tier outcomes become a focus only if there has been success at the higher levels (Figure 4.2). Tier 1 outcomes are "hard" clinical outcomes, with survival being the one of greatest importance for many conditions. Right below survival is the degree of

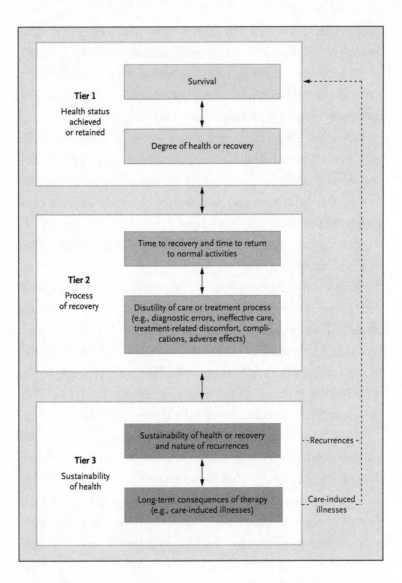

Figure 4.2   Michael Porter's three-tier outcomes measurement hierarchy
Reprinted from Michael E. Porter, "What Is Value in Health Care?" *New England Journal of Medicine* 363, December 23, 2010: 2477–2481.

health or recovery achieved, which can often be measured only by asking patients how they are doing. For example, virtually all hospitals have similar five-year survival rates for prostate cancer surgery (about 95 percent), but there is tremendous variation in outcomes such as incontinence and sexual dysfunction.

If a hospital is statistically worse than expected on Tier 1 outcomes, especially mortality, it faces a crisis that must be addressed as quickly as possible. However, it is difficult to clearly and consistently outperform other good providers on mortality and other Tier 1 outcomes. If a provider group is doing well on Tier 1 outcomes, it must then turn its attention to Tier 2 outcomes, which are related to the process of care.

The first level of Tier 2 outcomes reflects the time required to achieve recovery. These outcomes include delays and the disutility of care; such outcomes may not influence mortality but matter greatly to patients. Patient experience data dominate this tier of Porter's framework. Tier 3 outcomes reflect the durability of the benefits of a healthcare intervention. For example, a hip replacement that lasts 2 years is not the same as one that lasts 15 years.

The implied message of the switch from patient satisfaction to patient experience is that efforts aimed at improvement that focus solely on patients' perceptions of their service are not strategic investments of resources. Those patient satisfaction efforts may bring a temporary bump in volume, but they do not actually improve value, which is measured as outcomes versus the cost of providing those outcomes. Improvement of value for patients has to be the core of any viable long-term strategy for healthcare organizations.

Improvement of patient experience means getting better at meeting patients' needs, clinical as well as psychosocial. If clinicians feel skeptical and lack a visceral connection to patient satisfaction, they tend to resonate with improvement of patient experience and the concept of value once they grasp their meaning: meeting patients' needs as efficiently as possible.

Data show that patients have understood what was really important in healthcare all along. In analyses of the factors most strongly correlated with top ratings for hospitals, the following were at the top:

- How well the staff worked together

- Responsiveness to concerns and complaints

- Whether patients were included in decisions regarding their treatment

- Responsiveness to emotional needs

- Whether nurses kept patients informed

In these analyses, the quality and temperature of the food ranked near the very bottom, along with the courtesy of the person who served the food. Good "service behaviors" can be helpful in reducing patients' anxiety and stress, but patients seem to know that when they seek healthcare, they are not coming to a resort for recreation or a restaurant for a great meal.

Concerns About Patient Experience Data

If patient experience and other outcomes become the focus of healthcare delivery, it makes perfect sense that measuring patient experience and giving providers feedback on the results are essential. However, there is a problem: no one likes feedback that indicates that there is room for improvement.

This dynamic is part of the human condition and is summarized well in the book *Thanks for the Feedback: The Science and Art of Receiving Feedback Well.*[3] The authors, Douglas Stone and Sheila Heen, point out that we all receive feedback all the time but dread it and would rather dismiss than accept it. There is a basic conflict between our desire to improve and our desire to be appreciated and accepted as we are. Guess which one kicks in first most often.

Stone and Heen argue that we probably need to spend a bit less of our energy on perfecting the data and a bit more on preparing people to receive the feedback (actually, a *lot* more on the latter). In healthcare, that means recognizing that the first response to critical feedback is to look for reasons why the findings may be wrong. The second is to try to discredit the sources. To have these reflex reactions is to be human. The goal should be to recognize them in ourselves and not let them pose a barrier to using feedback to improve.

As you might imagine, my colleagues at Press Ganey and I hear criticisms, concerns, and skepticism about patient experience measurement all the time. Providers worry that the measures reflect hotel functions rather than the issues that determine patients' health outcomes. Also, they are concerned that the conclusions drawn from the data are not statistically valid because the sample sizes are too small and that the ability to adjust for variables that might skew the results is limited.

Some of these concerns are myths or are simply untrue. Others are real and need to be put in perspective while the problems are addressed. Fortunately, measurement is evolving in ways that are taking on these challenges and making the feedback on patient experience and other types of data more useful for driving an epidemic of empathy.

Adopting a framework from my colleague Deirdre Mylod, I divide these concerns into two groups. *Conceptual issues* include topics such as concern that greater patient satisfaction might be linked to worse outcomes and that measurement of patient experience might actually worsen care. *Data issues* are concerns about the validity of the information. Are enough data being collected? Are the results stable and statistically valid? Do they have meaning for individual physicians?

In effect, these common concerns represent feedback for organizations that collect patient experience data and for the provider leaders who use them. Clinicians should recognize that their reservations about patient experience data might be a reflection of the natural tendency to try to deflect feedback. However, my colleagues and I and provider leaders should similarly avoid the tendency to hastily dismiss these reservations and thus miss opportunities to improve.

Conceptual Issues

Does measuring patient experience have potentially perverse effects? This question is frequently raised by physicians who are concerned that their care is being evaluated on the basis of data collected from patients. Here are some examples of the issues they raise:

1. Medicine is complex, and patients do not have the training to know what is in their best interest. Therefore, patients' opinions of what constitutes good care are of uncertain value at best.

2. There are many patients who have strong but misguided ideas about what they need, for example, an MRI of their brains for a headache or antibiotics for a cold. Society's interests are best served by avoiding overuse or inappropriate use of such care, but withholding it may cause patients to rate their physicians poorly.

3. Some patients seek narcotic pain medications and will rate physicians poorly if those medications are withheld.

Critics argue that perverse consequences can result if too much attention is devoted to patient experience data, as if it were the only dimension of quality that mattered. They worry about unintended effects such as acceding to patients' requests for costly, inappropriate, and potentially harmful therapies if financial incentives are based on patient experience measures. Furthermore, critics worry that physicians are leaving their practices because of the intensity and potential perversity of pressures related to patient experience.

Is there evidence that physicians are being subjected to personal financial incentives that are focused on narrow targets, such as pain management? I have not found hospitals or physician groups tying compensation to changes in individual measures such as the percentage of patients who are satisfied with their pain management. If there were any, I would be critical of such an incentive.

Still, perception can be more powerful than reality. I recently asked an angry but thoughtful emergency medicine physician if he knew of any doctors who had a financial incentive that was based on patients' pain scores, if he knew doctors who gave narcotics or antibiotics to every patient who asked for them, or if he knew any physicians who had left the practice of medicine because they believed those measures were causing them to do the wrong thing. He agreed that he could not document that any of these assertions were true. "But," he said, "it feels like they are true."

In a sense, he was reflecting the duress that clinicians are under in the modern era of healthcare. That duress is real and causes physicians and others to latch on to any data that might undermine the validity of the feedback they are receiving.

One paper is brought up repeatedly as evidence that higher patient satisfaction may lead to worse care. A 2012 study published in the *Archives of Internal Medicine* was based on data on 51,946 adult respondents to the national Medical Expenditure Panel Survey from 2000 to 2007.[4] Researchers led by Joshua Fenton, MD, of the University of California, Davis, looked at data for each patient over a two-year period, including mortality through the end of 2006. Patient satisfaction was assessed with five items from the CAHPS survey from the first year, and correlations were sought with healthcare utilization in the second year.

The researchers found that patients in the highest quartile of patient satisfaction had lower rates of emergency department use, higher rates of hospitalization and medication use, greater total spending, and higher mortality compared with patients in the lowest quartile. The paper is often quoted as suggesting that higher patient satisfaction leads to higher death rates and higher costs.

The authors did not draw any such conclusion, of course. They noted the limitations in the data available to them. They could only work with five questions regarding patients' assessments of their primary care physicians' performance on specific activities (e.g., listening carefully, explaining things in a way that was easy to understand) and a global assessment of all their care from all physicians and providers on a scale of 0 to 10. These data were rolled together, with each item weighted equally, into a measure that was supposed to represent year 1 satisfaction. They could not look, for example, at whether patients' satisfaction with their hospital care correlated with hospital mortality.

If one reads the paper carefully and looks at the actual data in the tables, there is not a "dose-response" effect: a trend in which the higher the patient satisfaction, the higher the mortality. Yes, the patients in the highest quartile have the highest mortality, but the patients in the third quartile actually have slightly lower mortality than do the patients in the second quartile. If higher satisfaction led to worse outcomes, one would expect the opposite. The same is true for hospital admissions.

The authors understood the limitations of their data and their analysis and pointed out that "patient satisfaction may be a marker for illness, identifying patients who rely more on support from their physicians and thus report higher satisfaction." They expressed concern that excessive attention to patient satisfaction incentives may distract physicians, but in their concluding paragraph they wrote, "These associations warrant cautious interpretation and further evaluation, but they suggest that we may not fully understand the factors associated with patient satisfaction."

The caution they urge has not always been exercised by critics of patient experience measurement who quote their paper. Nevertheless, when I ask, "Do you really think that better communication with patients leads to higher hospital admission rates or increases mortality?" not one person has said yes.

The *Archives* paper is quoted so often in large part because it stands alone. The overwhelming findings from other research studies are in the opposite direction: better patient experience correlates with better quality and better patient outcomes. For example, the *New England Journal of Medicine* paper published in 2008 by Ashish Jha and colleagues from the Harvard School of Public Health analyzed the relationship between patient ratings of hospitals in the HCAHPS survey and other quality metrics related to hospitals. They found that hospitals in the top quartile of HCAHPS ratings had better performance on quality metrics for all four clinical conditions examined: acute myocardial infarction, congestive heart failure, pneumonia, and prevention of surgical complications.[5]

A study of more than 100,000 patients undergoing surgery by the American College of Surgeons National Surgical Quality Improvement Program analyzed the relationship between HCAHPS performance and well-documented clinical outcomes, including 30-day postoperative mortality, major and minor complications, and hospital readmission.[6] After adjusting for the extensive clinical data in their data set, the researchers found that hospitals in the top quartile in HCAHPS performance had a 15 percent reduction in risk of patient death compared with hospitals in the lowest quartile. Their conclusion: "Using a national sample of hospitals, we demonstrated a significant association between patient satisfaction scores and several objective measures of surgical quality.

Our findings suggest that payment policies that incentivize better patient experience do not require hospitals to sacrifice performance on other quality measures."

When this general topic—is patient experience related positively or negatively to actual patient outcomes?—was examined by researchers from Duke, they concluded that "patient experience measures provide robust measures of quality."[7] They shared others' skepticism that amenities improve patient outcomes but noted how the HCAHPS survey gets at activities that are at the core of good medicine. They cited as examples three specific questions from the survey:

- Question 3, from the section "Your Care from Nurses": During this hospital stay, how often did nurses explain things in a way you could understand? (Answer options: Never, Sometimes, Usually, Always).

- Question 17, from the section "Your Experiences in This Hospital": Before giving you any new medicine, how often did hospital staff describe possible side effects in a way you could understand? (Answer options: Never, Sometimes, Usually, Always)

- Question 20, from the section "When You Left the Hospital": During this hospital stay, did you get information in writing about what symptoms or health problems to look out for after you left the hospital?" (Answer options: Yes, No)

They thought such measures were powerful and intuitively valid measures of quality but noted that we have much to learn about how to collect and analyze the data.

On the specific issue of prescribing pain medication, there are no questions that patients with drug-seeking behavior exist, particularly in the emergency department setting. Not many of those patients actually complete patient experience surveys, but nevertheless, the fact that patient experience is being measured definitely crosses physicians' minds when they find themselves in conflict with patients. Regardless of how physicians may respond to this concern in individual cases, it is worth noting that a low threshold for prescribing narcotics would be a poor strategy for trying to raise one's patient experience scores.

First, a study of 4,749 emergency department patients showed no relationship between use of opioid analgesics and Press Ganey measures of patient experience.[8] If anything, there was a trend in the opposite direction: more narcotic use was associated with lower scores. Second, pain management did not figure at all in the analysis of the drivers of likelihood to recommend described in Chapter 2.

An analysis of data from emergency department patients shows that pain management is important to them, but after adjusting for data on communication, compassion, and coordination, the impact of pain management on the likelihood to recommend an emergency department is no longer statistically significant. If physicians are prescribing narcotics more freely in an attempt to improve their ratings or win their patients' loyalty, it is a poorly conceived strategy. What their patients actually want is compassionate, connected care, at the core of which is sensitivity to their physical and other types of suffering.

There are other studies showing that better patient experience scores correlate with lower hospital mortality,[9] better guideline adherence,[10] and better resource use.[11] Nevertheless, there is no denying that medicine is a complex activity, and conflicts between values within it abound. The best example may be the paper by my late friend and colleague Jane C. Weeks, MD, who described how many patients receiving chemotherapy for incurable cancers do not understand that the chemotherapy is unlikely to be curative. Her study showed that physicians who seemed to be more effective in communicating the true prognosis to their patients might be rated more poorly for their communication skills. In other words, physicians who were more truthful might have lower ratings of patient satisfaction.[12]

The findings in this paper should never be used as an argument for misleading patients about their prognosis in the pursuit of higher patient experience scores. Instead, the data demonstrate the complexity of medicine and the importance of adopting a nuanced approach to the use of the data. First, however, one must address the concerns about the data themselves.

Data Issues

Even if clinicians accept the idea that patient experience is important and is important to measure, they often cite an array of concerns about the data that are being collected and, they feel, used against them. Creating an environment in which clinicians feel that the goal is to improve care rather than judge them is of obvious importance, since data collection will never be complete and the ability to analyze data will never be perfect. However, to be realistic, clinicians will always feel somewhat judged by patient experience measurement, and every effort must be made to make that judgment feel fair.

The types of concerns most frequently articulated by clinicians include the following:

- The sample sizes are too small.

- The respondents are not representative of the overall population of patients who are receiving care from a clinician.

- The respondents really received care from many clinicians, and it is inappropriate to attribute the results to any one of them.

- The data are old, and care has changed in the interim.

- The scores fluctuate.

- The scores are too tightly packed; so many patients give high ratings that patient-reported data cannot be used to discriminate among providers.

- The interpretation of the data/benchmarking does not have adequate adjustment for risk factors that may account for lower performance.

- Analyzing and reporting data to describe the relative performance of physicians or hospitals leads to a harsh picture; for example, physicians with fairly high reliability (e.g., 90 percent or more) on a measure might be described as average or even below average.

All these concerns have a basis in reality, and they can all be addressed or mitigated through the approaches described in the remainder of this chapter. More data can be collected in a timelier manner if new data collection approaches are used. The ideal of collecting data from 100 percent of patients will probably never be realized, but when more data are collected in a timely way, the trends they reveal become hard to ignore.

Risk adjustment will never be complete, and so even if 100 percent of patients respond to surveys, comparisons among providers will always be susceptible to error. That is why it is so important that clinicians consider the goal of performance measurement as improvement: they are competing with themselves, trying to be better next year than they are now. Assuming that a physician's or hospital's patient mix is not changing dramatically, trying to compete with oneself sounds like a fair fight and a good goal. Opportunities to learn and improve can be highlighted through the use of appropriate benchmarks, such as comparing performance against similar organizations or against doctors with a similar specialty.

It is true that patients are generous graders and tend to give providers high marks (e.g., 80 percent of patients give physicians a 5 on a 5-point scale when asked about their likelihood of recommending them), an observation that belies concerns that only angry patients take the time to fill out surveys. That said, 20 percent do not give top ratings. Also, when data are analyzed across multiple measures, there are plenty of patients who do not give top marks on all aspects of care to hospitals or doctors. Top box analyses on all hospitals using HCAHPS between January 1, 2013, and June 30, 2014, show that almost a decade after HCAHPS was introduced, only 20 percent of patients reported that 100 percent of their needs were met. Nationwide, hospital inpatients report HCAHPS items at the individual attribute level as optimal between 49 percent and 89 percent of the time.

In short, no providers are perfect, and there are plenty of opportunities for improvement if the data are used to find them. How do we resolve the tension between our need to improve and the imperfections in the data? The answer involves improving the measures, getting more data, and using the data appropriately.

Improving Measures, Data, and Reporting

Part of the leadership challenge driving an epidemic of empathy in the pursuit of better care is cultural. Ideally, clinicians and other personnel should accept the following:

- The organization has a noble goal that trumps all other concerns (e.g., the reduction of suffering).

- The goal is improvement, not being ranked the best. No one is the best. Everyone has aspects of care that can be improved, and everyone is starting from scratch with the very next patient.

• The orientation is toward care in the future, not what has happened in the past. Resting on one's laurels is not an option in healthcare. Patients do not care what you did for those who came before them; they want relief of their present and future suffering. Data provide insight into opportunities for doing better.

• Measures and data will never be perfect. There will always be issues related to potentially perverse effects if measures are carried to an extreme (e.g., giving every patient narcotics). But the pursuit of that noble goal cannot be delayed until perfection in measurement and data collection is achieved. *Not* measuring would be a major strategic error. Fortunately, the organization uses common sense in the application of measures and data, mitigating those potentially perverse effects.

Acceptance of these cultural themes relies on good faith efforts by organizations to do all they can to make the measures and the data as good as they can be. Fortunately, tremendous progress in patient experience measurement and reporting is under way, enabling healthcare organizations to mitigate and even eliminate many of the most important concerns of clinicians. These advances allow clinicians to focus on the critical challenge—actually improving their care—rather than searching for weaknesses in the data that would provide a rationale for rejecting their implications. Examples are now available to show that modern era patient experience measurement can drive both patient-centered care and professional pride.

In sum, measurement of patient experience is imperfect and always will be. To use the resulting data to drive an epidemic of empathy, the right course is to make measurement better and more complete and use the data wisely. The key areas of improvement under way are the following:

1. Measuring what matters

2. Advances in data quantity and collection methods

3. Advances in data analysis

Measuring What Matters to Patients

The concept of patient-centered care is becoming increasingly clear to healthcare providers; it is nothing more and nothing less than organizing around meeting patients' needs. Patients' needs are not organized in patients' minds in accordance with the traditional structure of medicine, which is based on various types of clinical expertise such as surgery and gastroenterology. Patients are not focused on whether individual clinicians are competent or reliable in their various roles; patients assume this competence exists, and they are usually correct.

These points lead to a conclusion that is disruptive for the measurement of performance in healthcare: the spotlight should be on the patient, not the provider. Clinicians' reliability is important, of course, but it is a means to an end. The end is defined by whether patients' needs are met.

My colleagues and I think that the goal of reducing patient suffering is consistent with most organizational mission statements and the motivations of virtually all healthcare clinicians and other personnel. The word *suffering* is an emotional one, of course, and one reason to use it is that it compels a response. However, the goal of performance measurement is not to make clinicians feel guilty; it is to help them respond to patients' needs with reliability.

Can suffering be measured? What I learned from my career in clinical research is that if something is important, you will figure out how to measure it as well as possible. Even if the issue is difficult to measure, such as quality of life, pain, or functional status—the ability of people to do the things they want to do—you approach the issue with discipline and methodological rigor. You frequently need to collect data from many patients, knowing that they will give widely varying responses. But if you collect enough data and calculate the average, you will get valuable information.

The famous story of the British statistician Francis Galton and the oxen at the country fair offers valuable insight. In 1906, Galton went to the annual West of England Fat Stock and Poultry Exhibition and observed a competition in which people tried to guess what the weight of a fat ox would be after it was slaughtered and prepared for sale as meat. Nearly 800 people made guesses. Some were "experts" (butchers or farmers), but many were "non-experts" (regular citizens). The guesses varied widely, of course, but the average was only one pound off from the actual weight.

What Galton realized is that in any guess, there is information plus error. If that error is random and you average the responses from many people, the errors cancel out, and what you are left with is information. This insight is described in the book *The Wisdom of Crowds*, in which James Surowiecki shows how groups of people are often smarter than the smartest individual.

The implication for the measurement of suffering is that if this enormous, complex issue is broken down into various components and information is collected from enough patients, providers can understand how their patients are suffering and try to reduce that suffering. There are many different types of suffering, of course; physical pain is just one of them. Therefore, the first critical step toward measuring suffering is to break it down into various types of unmet needs so that providers can organize themselves to address them.

My colleague Deirdre Mylod has been a key thought leader behind work to deconstruct suffering. Patient suffering can be categorized as inherent to the patient's medical condition and associated treatment or as avoidable, resulting from dysfunction in the care delivery process[13] (see Table 4.1).

The inherent suffering that patients experience before and after receiving a diagnosis may be unavoidable because of their specific medical problems. The role of providers is to anticipate, detect, and mitigate that suffering. Pain, other symptoms, and loss of function are just a few types of inherent suffering. Fear, anxiety, and distress over loss of autonomy are also of enormous concern to patients, sometimes even more than pain itself.

Inherent suffering also encompasses the impact of treatment for the patient's condition. Medications and procedures can cause side effects, pain, discomfort, loss of function, and unwelcome changes in appearance even when they ultimately lead to recovery. Detecting and mitigating these side effects of treatment lead to improvement in Porter's Tier 2 outcomes, which were described earlier in this chapter. Some pain cannot be eliminated. Some procedures will always be uncomfortable. Often, what providers can do to mitigate such suffering is help patients understand what to expect so that they are not frightened by the unknown.

If inherent suffering is driven by patients' conditions and their necessary treatments, avoidable suffering has nothing to do with their diseases and everything to do with the way healthcare providers are organized. Poor coordination of care, excessive waits for appointments, uncertainty about what will happen next, and ineffective care transitions all erode patients' trust and lead to anxiety, frustration, and fear. All these dysfunctions are preventable even if they seem beyond the control of individual personnel.

Collecting data that distinguish inherent from avoidable sources of suffering allows organizations to understand where patient needs have not been met and provides insight into what

Table 4.1 Deconstructing Suffering: Sources and Examples

Unavoidable Suffering (Provider's Goal: Mitigate)	Avoidable Suffering (Provider's Goal: Eliminate)
Symptoms of disease including pain	Unnecessary pain resulting from failure to identify and treat the source
Loss of functioning (temporary or permanent) Side effects	Undesirable outcomes, such as hospital-acquired conditions and readmission due to failure to follow evidence-based practice
	Misdiagnosis, delay in diagnosis
Fear or anxiety regarding outcome of treatment Fear or anxiety due to unfamiliar processes, disruption in daily life, and loss of control	Fear or anxiety due to poor coordination and teamwork, lack of respect shown to patient, and loss of trust in providers
Fear or anxiety arising from the implications of the diagnosis for health and functioning	Unnecessary waits and delays in treatment Poor adherence to discharge instructions and medication regimens resulting from inadequate communications and coordination

steps need to be taken to close that gap. Current questionnaires that measure patient experience do not directly ask patients about their level of suffering. However, they do ask patients to evaluate attributes of care, and those measures demonstrate where patients view their care as optimal versus less than optimal.

Suboptimal experiences help providers understand where patients' needs are not being met. Table 4.2 organizes the measures into needs that stem from inherent suffering and from avoidable suffering. Although the examples are derived from the inpatient setting, the constructs are relevant to all types of patient care.

Table 4.2   Examples of Patient Needs in the Inpatient Setting

Inherent Patient Needs Arising from Disease and Treatment	Patient Needs That Stem from Dysfunction in Care Delivery
As part of having a health condition or receiving treatment, patients have a need for:	When dysfunction exists, patients develop a need for:
• Pain control	• Courteous/respectful interactions
• Skilled care providers	• Reduced wait times
• Preparation for discharge	• Comfortable environment
• Information	• Adequate amenities
• Personalization	• Service recovery
• Empathy	• Teamwork among care providers
• Choice	
• Privacy	
• Responsiveness	

For example, patients have an inherent need for information. Uncertainty is unnerving and causes suffering. Survey questions on the extent to which physicians and nurses kept patients informed, the clarity of the communication, and the effectiveness of conveying to patients the side effects and purposes of tests and treatments provide insight into how well this need is being met.

There is an important and fundamental difference between organizing patient experience data around provider reliability and organizing it around patients' unmet needs. With the former and more traditional approach, the analyses describe the overall reliability of physicians, nurses, and other personnel. With the latter, the data are analyzed around different types of patients' needs.

These needs vary with a patient's condition, of course. An emerging trend is to segment patients into groups defined by condition. Patients with the same condition tend to have shared needs that can be best met by multidisciplinary teams organized around that condition. For example, congestive heart failure (CHF) patients endure a chronic, progressive, yet unpredictable disease course that results in needs for information that are different from the needs of patients with other diagnoses. Being aware of differing needs can help clinicians communicate more effectively with CHF patients to help them better understand their diagnosis and care plans. Patients with Parkinson's disease, diabetes, and other chronic conditions also have specialized information needs. It is thus important to collect, analyze, and report data for the levels at which accountability can be created and improvement can occur.

Advances in Data Quantity and Collection Methods

If getting feedback is painful, getting feedback that is based on a small sample of patients can be enraging. To drive improvement rather than generate rage, we need more data on more patients, and those data should be timely. Ideally, patient experience data should be like a vital sign collected as part of routine care at every opportunity so that problems can be detected early and addressed.

That ideal may never be fully attainable, but the collection of data from patients is undergoing extraordinary change, as is the flow of information in every other sector of life. The traditional approach to collecting patient experience data has been to use mailed surveys or telephone a modest sample of patients. This approach enabled surveillance for major problems but not improvement.

Although many institutions still rely on telephone and mailed surveys (and CMS and other regulatory bodies still require data collection via these older methods), the clear trend is toward electronic data collection. Using e-mail and other electronic approaches to contact patients allows rapid and efficient data collection, and so an increasing number of hospitals and physician practices are trying to collect information from every patient after every encounter.

Of course, not every patient has e-mail or is comfortable with Internet web pages or mobile devices, although the conventional wisdom that the elderly do not use e-mail is incorrect. As the baby boomers age, they are changing the nature of being old, just as they have changed every other institution in which they have been involved. Statistical adjustments for differences in age and other factors in patient populations make it possible to compare electronic survey results with data collected with traditional methods so that provider organizations can tell if they are improving or losing ground.

Response rates to e-surveys are about the same as those for mailed questionnaires at roughly 20 percent. This percentage is higher in some patient subsets (family members whose loved ones experienced hospice care respond more than 60 percent of the time) and lower in others (emergency department patients respond about 11 percent of the time). However, the bottom line is that e-surveying allows the collection of many more data much more quickly. When physicians receive feedback that is based on 250 patients instead of 25, it is harder for them to dismiss the data even if the sample may never be perfectly representative of their entire patient population. The conversation changes from why the data should be ignored to what providers need to do to get better.

The timeliness of data collected electronically can be startling. As shown in Figure 4.3, about half the results obtained by e-surveys

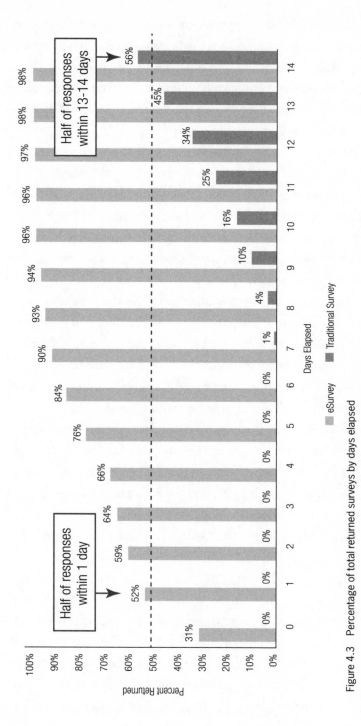

Figure 4.3   Percentage of total returned surveys by days elapsed

come in within a day, compared with about two weeks for mailed surveys. The freshness of e-survey data makes them that much more compelling to physicians and other healthcare personnel. Even though the surveys are anonymous, clinicians can often recall which patient was likely to have written the comments, making the feedback all the more real.

Another interesting difference is that with e-surveys, patients have a lower threshold for writing comments and tend to write longer comments. They frequently write paragraphs that paint a vivid picture of what they really appreciated or disliked about their care. These comments are proving to be compelling drivers of improvement for clinicians; no one would argue that risk adjustment is needed for such vignettes.

The success of collecting data electronically depends on an organization's active integration of e-mail capture into its operation. Organizations that have been effective at e-mail collection have embedded the process into their operations and have made it a clear priority with their staff. Some even give financial incentives to front-office staff for capturing e-mail addresses.

Research shows that organizations that capture more patient feedback tend to perform better because their data can be fully leveraged for quality improvement purposes. As depicted in Figure 4.4, regardless of hospital size, organizations that survey more than 81 percent of their patient populations see a higher average top box percentile ranking on the Overall Hospital Rating HCAHPS survey question compared with hospitals that surveyed fewer.

In summary, the clear direction is toward collection of data electronically from as many patients as possible. More data obtained more quickly help dispel some of the reasons clinicians might offer for ignoring recommendations that are based on patient experience data. To accelerate these trends, many organizations are starting to use point-of-care data collection, for example, using tablet computers to collect data from patients much more

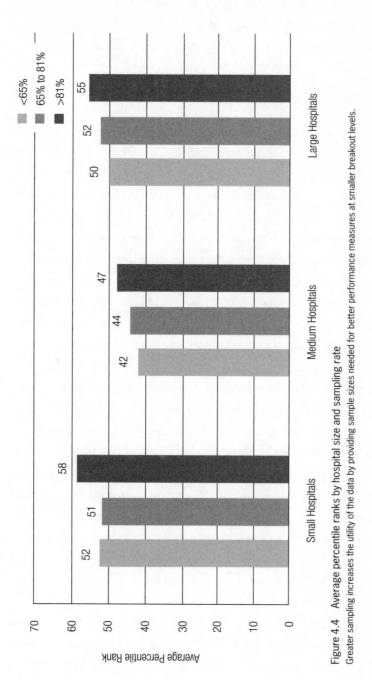

Figure 4.4 Average percentile ranks by hospital size and sampling rate

Greater sampling increases the utility of the data by providing sample sizes needed for better performance measures at smaller breakout levels.

frequently, such as every day or even every shift during a hospital-ization. These data can be used to overcome some of the challenges in attribution of information to individual clinicians.

Advances in Data Analysis

Collecting more data from more patients in a more timely fash-ion is the beginning of an ambitious agenda, not the end. Once those data are collected, they must be analyzed, put in context, and reported in ways that have an impact. As has been noted, the normal human response to feedback is to look for reasons why the findings may be wrong if those findings suggest the need for improvement. Even if patient experience and other types of quality data were collected from 100 percent of patients every day or every shift during hospitalizations, there would still be justifiable con-cerns about the use of those data to compare providers and decide who is best, who is merely average, and who is doing poorly.

Patients are individuals, of course, and just as two people may give drastically different reviews of the same movie, patients can walk away from the same healthcare experience with different impres-sions. One implication of this is that healthcare providers need to tune in to their patients as individuals and understand each of their needs and try to meet them; in other words, they need to practice empathy. Another is that healthcare providers need data on many patients so that the wisdom of crowds can be applied to the data and random errors caused by variation among individuals will cancel out.

However, just as individuals vary, so do groups. New Yorkers are tougher customers than Midwesterners. Younger patients are less likely to give top ratings than are older patients. Asians give fewer top grades than do European Americans. There are also complex systematic differences in interactions between groups of patients and groups of clinicians, for example, between patients and providers of different races or different genders.

The result of this complexity is that gathering tons of data doesn't automatically mean that apples-to-apples comparisons are easily done. Life is complicated, and so is healthcare. However, the fact is that benchmarking is valuable. It helps providers learn where there is opportunity to improve because someone out there is doing better. It helps providers learn when there is an imperative to improve because the data suggest that they may be doing worse than their colleagues.

The implication that emerges from Press Ganey's experience is that lots of data from lots of providers are necessary to do good benchmarking. National comparisons and benchmarking set the stage for understanding relative performance in a rapidly moving and increasingly competitive industry. Comparing groups of similar organizations—academic or community hospitals, organizations within the same state or city, organizations of like size or volume—refines the ability of providers to put their own performance in perspective. Similarly, using benchmarks that are specific to physician specialty or the type of care being provided can help account for differences in the underlying patient population, including their complexity, needs, and severity. The findings and trends may not change drastically with more detailed analyses, but they are often needed to overcome resistance to the feedback.

That said, even sophisticated analytics are not necessarily enough to drive improvement in performance, which requires feeding back data to units of accountability and units of improvement. Units of accountability are those which recognize responsibility for performance. Units of improvement are those which have the personnel and other ingredients needed to create permanent change for the better. Ideally, performance measurement provides the incentive and the road map for these units to improve.

To date, patient experience data are most effective when the units of accountability and improvement are the same, such as an individual physician in the outpatient setting. When individual physicians understand that they alone are responsible for demonstrating empathy to their patients and they get data and comments showing that there is room for improvement, there is a good chance that they will improve.

However, there are many issues that are important to patients for which individual clinicians do not feel accountable. For example, waiting time is a topic that often annoys physicians who are already working as hard as they can. (Their reaction is "What am I supposed to do? I am already seeing patients as quickly as I can for 12 hours a day.") Also, there are important issues such as the coordination of care, which depends on the actions of so many others, for which individual clinicians do not feel fully able to drive improvement.

For such issues, the problem is less the measures and the data and more the organization of care. A common observation these days is that healthcare is a team sport. But often the teams do not actually exist or the team members do not know that they are part of a team. In other words, there is no individual who feels accountable for performance, and there is no identifiable team either. Patient experience data can be collected, but when they are sent to healthcare organizations, they might as well be returned with the stamped message "Addressee Unknown."

An example I have observed at several hospitalist programs around the country goes something like this: The individual hospitalist physicians say that they want to be held accountable for their performance as individuals. However, in general, patients are surveyed at the end of a hospitalization, and the data are analyzed on the basis of the last physician who was overseeing the patient's care. The discharging physician may have been responsible for much of the patient's care or for very little. Frequently, the real action of the hospitalization occurred on someone else's watch.

Two potential solutions seem obvious, and both are needed. One is for the group of hospitalists to feel collective responsibility for their performance and to recognize that they are a team in which no individual's performance stands alone. The other is to collect more data throughout a hospitalization so that patients can be asked to give feedback on the care of the physicians, nurses, and other personnel with whom they have interacted during the last day or even the last shift. Some organizations are already moving in this direction, using tablet computers with photographs of the various personnel to help patients identify them.

The attribution challenge exists almost everywhere in medicine because teamwork is so essential to state-of-the-art healthcare delivery. In emergency departments, for example, patients with problems of any complexity often require care for more than one shift of clinical personnel. The response rates are already lower for emergency department patients than they are in other settings. Physicians can be irritated at getting feedback on a small number of patients for whom they don't feel ownership.

In such settings, cultivating the sense of group ownership is critical, and for patient segments with similar shared needs, a powerful new concept of the group is emerging. Integrated practice units (IPUs) are emerging in healthcare systems around the world in which multidisciplinary teams work to improve the value of care for patients with specific conditions such as prostate cancer and headache or those who need to undergo major surgical procedures such as cardiac or orthopedic operations.

These IPUs meet frequently and are often a more important focus for organizational identity for the clinicians than are the hospital departments that reflect their expertise. These teams exist to meet patients' needs and to do so efficiently. They hunger for data to help them, including the following:

- Patient reported outcomes measures (PROMs)

- Traditional quality metrics on the reliability with which key processes are occurring

- Cost data

- Personnel "engagement" data that capture how well the team is working as a team

All these types of data are important, and they interact with one another to influence patients' overall outcomes, experience, and costs. For example, more engaged teams are less likely to have turnover of personnel and thus avoid the costs and disruption of hiring and training replacements. Thus, creating real teams and giving them a fully integrated package of the data that they need to improve value are important goals for forward-looking organizations. Consolidating care of patients with target conditions with these IPUs will make the data more robust and increase the impact of such teams.

In sum, recent years have seen marked advances in the ability to measure what matters to patients. More data can be collected more quickly, and there is increasing clarity about their importance and how they should be analyzed. Nonetheless, the fact is that data are necessary but not sufficient to drive improvement. There has to be an organization and individuals within the organization who want to use the data to improve. These dynamics are the focus of the remainder of this book.

5 Social Capital and Social Network Science Come of Age

WE KNOW THE problem: the chaos and the resulting loss of empathy that are so common in modern medicine. We understand the strategic business imperative to improve: we are entering a healthcare marketplace driven by competition on value to the patient. That marketplace demands relentless efforts to improve the effectiveness and efficiency with which providers meet patients' needs. We grasp that empathic care is critical to meeting the needs of patients and appreciate that the science and technology related to measuring those needs is advancing. We know what we need to accomplish, and we are getting much better at measuring how we are doing.

But how do we actually do it? How do we spread the values that are reflected by what we are measuring? How do we make empathetic, coordinated care the norm rather than something akin to stars coming into alignment? How do we help individuals and groups of individuals in healthcare be at their best consistently and live up to their own aspirations for the care that they deliver to every patient every time?

Making progress toward this lofty goal requires understanding the importance of social capital, and amassing social capital requires thoughtful use of social network science. The insights that flow from research in both areas can strengthen the ability of healthcare organizations to compete and thrive in the new healthcare marketplace while bringing professional pride to their personnel and driving an epidemic of empathic care.

Social Capital

When healthcare organizations talk about capital, they are usually referring to financial capital: the monetary resources that enable organizations to erect buildings, buy equipment, and accomplish other goals that otherwise would be beyond their reach. They also may be referring to human capital, which is the intellectual quality of their doctors, nurses, and other personnel. Social capital is about coordinating the two. Social capital describes the advantages created through the structure and function of relationships both within the organization and with others outside the organization. Those relationships enable an organization to do things it couldn't otherwise do, such as reliably deliver care that is compassionate and coordinated.

Social capital explains why some organizations do a better job than others at meeting patients' needs and why other organizations so often fall short even though their personnel are every bit as intelligent and work just as hard. The higher-performing organizations do a better job and are more reliable because of the ways in which their personnel relate to one another both formally and informally. Teamwork is not an abstraction but a core part of the professional lives of their personnel.

Those medical professionals know what they are supposed to do as individuals and also what others are expected to do. There is trust among them, so rework can be minimized. There is a shared goal, so the most efficient way to accomplish that goal can be pursued collectively. There are norms that are not likely to be lightly violated, and one of those norms is putting the needs of patients above all other priorities.

A clear and useful framework for thinking about social capital can be found in the work of the University of Chicago sociologist Ronald S. Burt. Burt describes two basic ways in which organizations increase their social capital: brokerage and closure. Brokerage describes the way organizations learn and actually *increase* the variation in how they do things. Closure describes how they *reduce* variation and achieve consistency in working together in an effective and efficient way.

Organizations need both types of functions to drive an epidemic of empathy. They need to learn what others are doing to redefine what it means to meet patients' needs, such as using transparency with patients' comments to drive improvement, doing root-cause analyses when patients suffer a loss of dignity, and providing communications training programs to help clinicians learn what messages best encourage and convey empathy. That is information brokering. After learning about and piloting new ideas, personnel need closure to make those ideas the local norm.

Brokerage

Healthcare organizations are made up of people, and even though some people leave the organization every year and new ones enter, there is a history to the group of people. Within the organization, there are subgroups, and there are other organizations in the great beyond, all with their own histories and norms.

At my hospital in Boston, my colleagues and I are dimly aware that the Mayo Clinic has a social norm in which everyone answers his or her beeper right away. We don't talk about it every day. It comes up a couple of times a year after someone has visited Mayo

Clinic. He or she will say, "Do you know that they all answer their beepers immediately?" "Really?" we tend to say. "I think I've heard that before."

We have also heard that Cleveland Clinic asks every patient who calls seeking an appointment whether he or she would like to be seen that day. We point out that we see a large percentage of our patients on the same day they call and believe that we find a way to squeeze in virtually everyone who needs care urgently. But we do not guarantee same-day access, and we don't ask all patients if they want to be seen the same day. Nevertheless, we are aware that Cleveland Clinic and some other places in other cities are doing just that.

We were startled when we heard that the physicians at University of Utah Health Care were posting all their patients' comments on their find-a-doctor pages on the Internet. I remember that I was in the back row of a classroom at Harvard Business School in January 2013 when I first heard that from its CEO, Vivian Lee. My actual words to her were "You are kidding me!" (In my mind, I put an expletive before the word *kidding*.) Some of us went to the website to see if it was true. It was.

Although those examples were impressive, we didn't try to emulate them. We went back to the hard work of doing our job the way we always did it.

My colleagues and I tend to get a bit more concerned when we hear about different ways of doing things among colleagues closer to home, especially in the Boston area. After all, they are our competitors and our friends. Our children go to school together. Our patients live in the same communities and often go back and forth among our institutions. Therefore, when one hospital, Beth Israel Deaconess, began giving patients full access to their medical records through a program called OpenNotes, the clinicians in other hospitals could not help but sit up and pay attention.

My colleagues at Boston's academic medical centers are aware that there are organizations around the country that are a lot like ours. My colleagues at Brigham and Women's Hospital take note when they hear about changes in the design of care at academic medical centers such as Johns Hopkins, Yale, and Stanford. My colleagues at Boston's safety-net hospital, Boston Medical Center, are in touch with their counterparts around the country. My colleagues at Dana-Farber Cancer Institute are carefully watching what goes on at other comprehensive cancer centers. We are all aware of the community in which we work and the broader communities that are relevant to us. There is variation in the way things are done within and across these communities. Some ways of doing things are better than others in meeting patients' needs effectively and efficiently. Some are clearly best practices.

Variation provides an opportunity to improve by learning. How quickly and reliably are these various practices compared, and how quickly and reliably do the best practices emerge and spread? The efficiency of this market of ideas is determined by organizations' effectiveness at information brokering.

As attractive as the idea of spreading best practices sounds, the reality is that the barriers to doing this are considerable. Burt writes, "When people specialize on their immediate tasks to the exclusion of adjacent tasks, they lose track of other groups and the external environment. Variation in belief and practice develops between groups. People here do it differently than people over there. In fact, in-group communication can create barriers to information inconsistent with prevailing beliefs and practice."[1]

In other words, the more intense and inward-facing a culture is, the harder it is for information from the outside to penetrate. That observation is consistent with a self-deprecating joke about the medical community in which I practice: "Over the years, many great ideas have come out of Harvard, but very few have gotten in."

The problem of insularity demands a conscious, systematic effort to learn from the outside.

Burt writes about people working in clusters and the importance of bridges between those clusters so that information can reach them. It is one thing to hear that the physicians at Geisinger Health System do things a certain way; it's another thing to actually go to Danville, Pennsylvania, and see them in action. In the former context, it is too easy to dismiss the description of some best practices with the casual remark "They are organized differently from us."

However, by visiting, you cross the bridge between clusters. You may find that in some ways the other institution is different but that the commonalities with your institution are actually strong. Their heart-failure patients also show up short of breath; their elderly patients also have trouble keeping track of 18 medications; their pediatric patients also have worried parents. The patients' problems are the same, and many of the solutions from Geisinger or Mayo or Cleveland Clinic or Intermountain could easily be adopted elsewhere.

The truth is that there are practices to emulate almost everywhere you look—if you are looking for them. Here is one of my favorites. At Novant Health in North Carolina, clinicians have developed a Code Comfort protocol in which the needs of dying patients who are short of breath or in pain are met with the same intensity, discipline, and urgency as a cardiac arrest, or Code Blue. We are talking about patients who are not candidates for a transfer to the intensive care unit or for cardiopulmonary resuscitation.

At most hospitals, when such patients get short of breath or are in pain, the nurses page the doctors and the doctors phone in an order to increase narcotics and antianxiety medicines. Sometimes those measures are enough; sometimes they are not. The physician is often tied up with patients who are perceived as having "more active issues" because they are more likely to survive. The nurses are on their own with the dying patients in distress.

Novant's leadership didn't want patients, their families, or the nurses to feel helpless in these situations. They laid out clear steps for relieving pain and shortness of breath by increasing medications and enabled nurses to increase medications to relieve the suffering of patients without a physician's order, just as they can use a defibrillator if a patient has a cardiac arrest.[2]

If these steps do not ease the patient's symptoms, the nurses can call a Code Comfort in the same way they might call a Code Blue. In this case, the clinicians who come running are pain specialists and other personnel who are expert in relieving the suffering of dying patients. The development of the clear protocols has made the need for calling Code Comforts rare. The nurses and the families of dying patients get peace of mind just from knowing that the Code Comfort option exists.

Other organizations are imitating the Code Comfort program, and the whole initiative has brought Novant national attention and pride. These other organizations do not ask to see randomized controlled trial data demonstrating that the Code Comfort initiative improves some outcome metric. They learned about it by word of mouth and through a description on the *Harvard Business Review* website posted on December 9, 2014. The story did not take long to find its audience. Fiercehealthcare.com ran an article on December 11; theadvisory-board.com, on December 12; and forbes.com, on December 13.

Once the information was out there, why did some organizations absorb the idea and start to imitate it whereas others did not? As Burt writes, organizations can strengthen themselves by creating "holes" through which information can enter and building bridges by which information can move from one group to another. If these holes and bridges are planned and important features of organizational life, there is a better chance that a good new idea will be recognized and adopted. In contrast, if bridges and holes to the outside world are not prominent in an organization and its leaders are preoccupied with listening to one another, the variation that is necessary for improvement happens more slowly, if at all.

For this reason, healthcare organizations seeking to drive an epidemic of empathy should do what they can to be part of the larger healthcare community that shares the same goal. When colleagues from different organizations spend time with one another even in informal settings, unintentional learning can occur. For example, I learned about Mayo's cultural norm of promptly answering beeper pages during a taxi ride with a Mayo Clinic radiologist at a medical meeting. The only reason we were sharing a taxi was that it was raining and the line of people waiting for taxis was so long. A doorman suggested that we might share a cab since we were going to the same place; otherwise, we both would have ridden alone, and my learning would not have occurred.

Burt describes four levels of brokerage through which value can be created:

1. The simplest is to make people in two different organizations aware of the interests and challenges in each other's settings. In healthcare, common ground can virtually always be identified quickly, since the goal every organization shares is meeting the needs of its patients. Sick people everywhere are in pain and worried; healthy people everywhere are hoping to stay healthy.

2. Transferring best practices is a higher level of brokerage. When an organization adapts something that is creating value in another organization, that effort has a better chance of success than does a completely original idea because the "stolen" concept has already been tested. For this reason, a colleague and I have (half jokingly, but only half) recommended the formation of a healthcare Institute for Imitation as opposed to innovation.[3]

3. Drawing analogies between two groups that seem to be irrelevant to each other can lead to creative solutions to patients' problems. For example, awareness that banking and retailers are meeting consumers' needs 24/7 suggests that forward-looking healthcare providers should consider doing the same thing. Similarly, understanding that the military is able to entrust 21-year-old youths with nuclear submarines and other complex devices suggests that lessons might be learned from those services that could make healthcare delivery safer. In healthcare, social capital can be created simply by recognizing that perceived cultural differences between provider organizations are not as vast as imagined and that best practices at one can be adapted at another.

4. Synthesis is the highest form of brokerage: creating something new that doesn't exist on either side of the bridge, combining strengths and concepts seen in both groups.

In sum, brokerage leads to learning and fosters improvement through both imitation and innovation. Brokerage can happen by accident—like my taxi ride with the Mayo Clinic physician—or it can be promoted systematically. Organizations that are inwardly focused are obviously at higher risk of falling behind and losing out in a competitive environment because they are slower to learn and change.

However, brokerage is just one part of the creation of social capital. For the ideas that flow from brokerage to achieve their full effect, organizations have to take on the challenging work of closure.

Closure

Almost every organization has people who are eager to innovate. They like to visit other places, and they come back bubbling with new ideas. They are the brokers. Almost every organization also has respected and trusted individuals who are watched closely and emulated by others. Frequently, they are the leaders who can create closure, in which controversy and variation around a practice fade away and that practice becomes the norm within the group.

To enable the dissemination and adoption of a powerful idea, such as an epidemic of empathy, organizations need to integrate their abilities to learn and to trust. Learning allows brokerage, and trust enables closure. A new idea (e.g., we should take the time with each patient to ensure that we understand his or her needs) is introduced, and trust enables the group to function like a team and commit to standardizing the practice and thus reach closure.

Powerful ideas have a way of spreading, but they spread much faster and more effectively in organizations in which people trust one another. It takes trust to adopt ideas from elsewhere at the suggestion of a colleague who has seen them in action and says that they lead to better care. It takes trust to work like a real team, one in which you can depend on others to do their jobs so that you don't have to check and recheck their work. It takes trust to know that if you make the extra effort to deliver compassionate care and coordinate your work with that of others, your colleagues will do the same thing.

As Burt writes, "Trust is a relationship with someone (or something if the object of trust is a group, organization, or social category) in which contractual terms are incompletely specified. The more unspecified, taken-for-granted, the terms, the more that trust is involved. You anticipate cooperation from the other person, but you commit to the relationship before you know how the other person will behave."[4]

Leaders who are effective in driving closure in an organization tend to be those who have earned trust from their colleagues over time. Without such trusted closure leaders, the potential value created by information brokers who have brought ideas across the bridges cannot be translated into social capital. Here is a simple example. Many healthcare organizations started considering full public transparency of their patient experience data after University of Utah Health Care introduced the concept in 2013. However, the organizations that have moved ahead more quickly and implemented this approach tend to be those with a strong physician leader who endorsed it and helped create a review system that clinicians trusted would be fair and would be aimed at improvement rather than humiliation.

Trust is more easily cultivated and closure more easily achieved in organizations that are "tight," that is, organizations in which personnel know one another and have regular formal and informal interactions and deviations from the norm are easily noticed and acted on. For example, in a small group practice, a clinician who does not deliver care with empathy—or any other dimension of quality—is easily detected. The question is whether the group will exercise its advantage and use its social capital to enforce the social norm of expected excellence.

The value of closure is realized only when such variation is reduced. Even though detection of variation (e.g., poor performance on some dimension of quality, including patient experience) is easier in a small group, that detection is possible with systematic efforts in large organizations, and effective programs to reduce variation can be implemented even without the use of financial incentives. However, this requires effective systems of accountability, which are discussed more directly in Chapter 6.

Let's close this section with an audacious suggestion with implications for boards and senior management: cultivation of social capital may be more important to the success of healthcare organizations today than amassing financial capital is. I'm not naive about the importance of money, but you can borrow money, whereas you cannot borrow culture or the loyalty of patients drawn to care that is coordinated and empathic. To provide the care required to be competitive in a value-drive marketplace, organizations must be able to innovate, learn, and work in teams. The ability to consider ideas from outside the group, decide which ones to adopt, and standardize care around the new ideas will be a competitive differentiator.

Let us turn to the question of how social capital can be used with advances in social network science to drive an epidemic of empathy.

Social Network Science

Social capital provides broad insights into what organizations need to do to improve performance in this era in which medicine is so complex, so much a team sport, and so expensive. These organizations need to encourage variation in their communities through brokerage—that is, trying new ways of working and working together—but they also have to be ready to *decrease* variation through closure and promote standardization when that will improve the quality and/or efficiency of care.

Social network science provides insights into how the spread of the values and social norms occurs. Researchers such as Nicholas Christakis and James H. Fowler, the authors of *Connected: The Surprising Power of Our Social Networks and How They Shape Our Lives,*[5] have done much more than describe the structure of communities defined by membership on Facebook or LinkedIn. They have shown how networks function almost like organisms and have characterized the "physiology" through which values spread within them. Their work provides a game plan for healthcare organizations that want to make empathetic, coordinated care a basic value among all their personnel not just some of the time but for every single patient.

Contagious Behavior: An Example

Do behaviors, emotions, and values really spread in the same patterns as infectious disease, from person to person to person? Sometimes the effects of social networks look exactly like those of an infectious condition. For example, in August 2011, Katie Krautwurst developed facial tics. At that time, she was a high school cheerleader in Le Roy, New York, a small town in the western part of that state. Within weeks, her best friend, Thera Sanchez, was displaying similar tics as well as stuttering and involuntary arm movements. Soon a third cheerleader was exhibiting symptoms like Thera's. By midwinter, 18 residents of Le Roy were in the thrall of the mysterious disorder, including one male high school student and a 36-year-old nurse.

An early skeptical voice was that of Laszlo Mechtler, a neurologist who treated 15 of the girls at the Dent Neurologic Institute, about an hour away from Le Roy. He diagnosed the mysterious epidemic as conversion disorder: the development of neurologic symptoms, including involuntary motion, facial and vocal tics, paralysis, and seizures, without an identifiable physical cause. Neurologists and psychiatrists believe that conversion disorders are generated by psychological stress that is expressed in physical symptoms.

Mechtler's diagnosis was disputed by many of the patients, their parents, and community leaders. They called in the environmental activist Erin Brockovich to investigate toxic-waste emissions as a possible cause. Brokovich's investigation failed to find any connection between her prime environmental suspect—a 1970 chemical spill—and the teens' symptoms. Investigators from the Environmental Protection Agency and the New York State Environmental Commission also came up empty-handed.[6]

By January 2012, the national media had caught wind of the mysterious epidemic and some of the girls had been interviewed on *Today* and *Dr. Drew*. They captured the attention of a pediatric neurologist, Rosario Trifiletti, who specializes in a rare condition called pediatric autoimmune neuropsychiatric disorder associated with streptococcus (PANDAS). Trifiletti saw a possible PANDAS outbreak and volunteered to consult with the families of the affected teens. Several signed on as his patients. Although their blood tests for strep antigens were inconclusive, he prescribed antibiotics and anti-inflammatories. In contrast, those who stuck with Mechtler were referred to talk therapy.

During their treatments, the girls were posting updates about their condition on Facebook. Some also uploaded videos showing their tics and spasms to YouTube. The local and national media persisted in their coverage throughout the school year. Some teens began to show improvement from their treatments, with the greatest improvement apparent in those at the periphery of the epidemic: the youths who were not in Krautwurst's and Sanchez's inner circle but who may have shared a class with one of them. Those youths had also escaped the media spotlight.

By late winter, all the affected youths were doing better. Their tics had abated, and some were able to resume cheerleading and other activities. Whether the antibiotics or talk therapy had helped was still a subject of debate. Neither treatment seemed to be as strongly related to improvement as much as another factor: the cessation of media coverage. Once attention was diverted from the epidemic, most of the affected teens started to recover.

As Mechtler explained in a British documentary *The Town That Caught Tourette's*, "One of the ways we know to treat this problem is to restore normality—not just to the individual but to the community. But every time a patient would come to me doing better, all it would take is for them to turn on the TV or be approached by the media to aggravate their symptoms."[7]

Although Mechtler and his colleague Jennifer McTige had seen many cases of conversion disorder, this was the first time they had witnessed an epidemic of it, a situation known as mass psychogenic illness. They posited that Katie Krautwurst, the index case, had been under stress from her mother's repeated brain surgeries. Her close friends had responded to her tics and twitches by unconsciously mirroring them. Susceptible students who shared classes with the affected girls were similarly stricken. Even the afflicted nurse was a close friend of a parent of one of the teens.

Bringing Science to the Study of Social Networks

At the Yale Institute for Network Science, Christakis and his colleagues have been studying how social networks work; their insights help explain episodes such as the Le Roy incident and also provide guidance on how to drive an epidemic of empathy. These are certainly not the only social network scientists making important contributions today, but their work is often directly relevant to healthcare delivery, reflecting Christakis's background as a palliative care physician.

Christakis stumbled into the field of network science 20 years ago, when he was a hospice physician studying the "widower" effect: the increased risk of dying "of a broken heart" after the passing of a spouse. As one of his patients was dying of dementia, Christakis noted that as expected, there was a terrible toll on her husband, her daughter, and the daughter's husband. The younger generation was worried both for the patient and for the soon-to-be widower. Christakis was taken aback when he got a phone call from one of the son-in-law's friends, who described how the son-in-law's distress was casting a pall over the caller's life. The caller had never met the woman with dementia—in fact, he was three degrees of separation from her—but her illness was making him sick, too.

At that time, national alarm was intensifying over the increase in obesity, which had doubled over the previous two decades. Public health officials began to talk of an obesity epidemic sweeping the country. If there was indeed an epidemic, Christakis reasoned, he should be able to track its spread.

Christakis and his colleague, the political scientist James Fowler of the University of California, San Diego, found the ideal population in which to track obesity: the Framingham Offspring Study, a database of 5,124 people—all of them offspring of participants in the Framingham Heart Study—who had been examined seven times between 1971 and 2003. At each examination, the participants were weighed and asked to list their parents, spouses, siblings, and children. Here is the remarkable part of the Framingham database: the research subjects were also asked to list the name of at least one close friend. In addition, the participants' addresses were updated frequently, and so the researchers knew how close they lived to one another.

Christakis and Fowler found that many of the friends and relatives named were also members of a Framingham study, and so there were data on them as well. The researchers were able to map network links among the participants at each examination and from one examination to the next. They were able to plot network dynamics over time: changes that were due to birth and death, the formation of new links through friendship and marriage, and links dissolved by relocation and divorce.

They found that having a friend who became obese increased one's chances of becoming obese by 57 percent. The effect was even greater for mutual friends: pairs of participants who named each other as a friend. It was greatest in friends of the same sex. In fact, a close friend might be more likely to influence one's weight than was a spouse. If a woman's husband's body mass index (BMI) topped 30, the chance that hers might follow suit was 37 percent. It was 40 percent if a sibling became obese. The authors published the study in the *New England Journal of Medicine* in 2007.[8]

The analysis seemed to rule out a host of factors that might have been responsible, including one of those most often blamed for the obesity epidemic: a change in the eating habits or availability of food in the community at large, such as a fantastic doughnut shop opening in the neighborhood. People didn't gain weight at the same time as their neighbors. In fact, social ties were much stronger influences than was geographic proximity. Friends who lived hundreds of miles away had the same effect on their friends' weight as did those who lived next door, whereas neighbors who weren't friends had no effect.

Christakis and Fowler postulated that the influence wasn't due to homophily, or "the birds of a feather flock together" effect. Obese people weren't likely to be linked as friends initially. In other words, they didn't seem to be attracted to one another because they felt comfortable or shared a love of food. One or both of a pair of friends became obese over time, and not necessarily at the same time.

Their evidence indicates that obesity became normalized in networks of friends. Having a friend of a friend become obese raised one's chance of becoming obese by 20 percent. Christakis suggests that this effect is due to subtle changes in attitude. Here's how it might work: You and Amy have been friends for a long time. You have lunch every couple of weeks, and Amy's disapproving glance keeps you from ordering dessert. Amy also lunches with Sheila, a friend from childhood whom you don't know. Sheila has been gaining weight gradually, and now she's obese. Amy has become accustomed to seeing Sheila as a larger woman who thoroughly enjoys her food, and she appreciates Sheila's healthy self-image. During one of your lunches, you order dessert and Amy doesn't react. She's become accustomed to eating with Sheila and has started to interpret overeating as having a healthy appetite. Soon you're ordering dessert every time you eat out.

In that 2007 study, the effect declined with more distant relationships but was still present at a third degree of separation. Having a friend of a friend of a friend become obese is associated with a 10 percent increase in a person's risk of obesity. Christakis refers to this as the Three Degrees of Influence Rule. Those authors have since shown, using a variety of ingenious experiments involving thousands and even millions of people, both online and offline, that findings similar to those in their observational studies can be documented with respect to behaviors as diverse as cooperation and vitamin use.

Christakis and Fowler's study was controversial not just because they concluded that obesity is a contagious disease but also because of some of the analytic methods they employed. They responded to their critics in a paper published by *Statistics in Medicine* in February 2013.[9] They also used alternative methods suggested by their critics in a December 2013 analysis tracing divorce through the Framingham cohort and came up with similar findings: Having a divorcing friend increases the likelihood that you and your spouse will split up. The likelihood was 75 percent if your own friends divorced and 33 percent if your friends' friends split up. There was no association farther down the network.[10]

Rules of Life in the Network

From their study of many social networks and by observing the spread of norms and social values, Christakis and his coauthor have described "Rules of Life in the Network." They begin by pointing out two fundamental aspects of the network, the first of which is the connections themselves: who has ties to whom and how strong and durable those ties are. The patterns are important as well. That is, if you have three friends, that is great. But if those three friends also have relationships among them, you have a stronger social network around you, and a new norm such as an epidemic of empathy may spread more quickly.

The second aspect is contagion, which they define as "*what*, if anything, flows across the ties.... [It] could be germs, money, violence, fashions, kidneys, happiness, or obesity. Each of these flows might behave according to its own rules."[11] They then define several rules that characterized the ways networks actually work.

Rule 1: We Shape Our Network

We choose whom we want to have in our network, how many close relationships we will have, and how they will be organized. In a survey of 3,000 randomly sampled Americans, Christakis and his colleagues found that people have just four close social contacts on average, with most having between two and six. In that survey, 12 percent of respondents listed no one with whom they could discuss important matters or spend free time and 5 percent had eight such people. Other researchers have found that the "core discussion networks" of Americans tend to decrease with age, that there is no difference between the sexes, and that college-educated Americans have core discussion networks nearly twice as large as those who do not graduate from high school.

In Christakis's work, his team next asks people how interconnected their social contacts are with one another. If their contacts also have close relationships, there is greater transitivity. Some people live in a tightly woven network in which everyone knows everyone, whereas people who live in low-transitivity networks may have multiple contacts but those contacts come from different subgroups of the world around them.

In healthcare, the issues raised by this rule include how connected the groups of personnel taking care of patients are. Do they actually know one another? Refer to Figure 2.1 in Chapter 2, which shows how important the coordination of care is to patients. If patients feel that they have a real team rather than a loosely connected group that Michael Porter likes to call a pickup team, those patients have greater peace of mind, and a reasonable assumption is that they are more likely to recommend the providers to others.

Real teams are in many ways the antidote to the chaos of modern medicine. Real teams meet to improve the care they provide. They meet formally to discuss their performance data and what they can and should do to improve. They meet informally, bumping into one another in the hallways or chatting at social gatherings. When they meet informally, they often discuss the care of individual patients, and the care of those patients is better because of those interactions. On real teams, there are clear roles and everyone knows what the others are doing and what he or she is going to do.

Rule 2: Our Networks Shape Us

Individuals turn out differently as a result of their environments. Firstborn children are different from their younger siblings in statistically significant ways. They don't all fit the stereotypes of eldest children, but there is a reason the stereotypes exist.

The transitivity of individuals' social networks can change outcomes. For example, one of my colleagues and his wife met in high school. They dated for a while, but she broke it off. By that point, however, he had become good friends with her brothers and parents, and they would routinely invite him over for Sunday dinner. Once he even brought his new girlfriend with him. After high school graduation, they went to the same college and resumed dating. They married when she was a senior, and three decades and three children later, things seem to have worked out just fine. Would there have been this outcome if she hadn't had a big, happy welcoming family that took him in and didn't let him go even after she broke things off? Probably not.

For healthcare providers, this rule has implications for real teamwork. If information can easily hop from person to person to person ("Mrs. Chan is worried about her knee surgery, but she is *really* worried about how her husband with Alzheimer's is going to do while she is laid up"), one can imagine how much more likely it is for care to be both coordinated and empathetic.

Rule 3: Our Friends Affect Us

What flows around the network can be negative (e.g., racist ideology) or positive (e.g., studious habits, aversion to litter, even happiness). Christakis points out that social networks are agnostic: they can spread both good things and bad things. In healthcare, the implication is that we should highlight positive examples in an effort to make them the norm.

For example, my colleagues at Brigham and Women's Hospital and I started a series in 2013 in which we put a physician-patient pair with a wonderful relationship on stage and interviewed them about what made the relationship so valuable to each of them. The format was modeled after the interviews of couples that are interspersed through the movie *When Harry Met Sally*. My Press Ganey colleagues and I have now done the same type of session elsewhere, and we have called this series "Love Stories." The questions we ask the pair are the kinds of questions you might ask two spouses: "How did you meet?" "What was your first impression?" and "How did you know it was going to be good?"

From these sessions, I have been reminded of just how rewarding a good doctor-patient relationship can be for both parties. I also have learned little tips, such as specific questions and comments that clinicians can use to convey that they understand patients' issues and are going to stick with them all the way and see them through.

Rule 4: Our Friends' Friends' Friends Affect Us

Christakis and his colleagues have shown that norms and behaviors spread in more complex ways than one individual infecting another or passing information on to another. Reinforcement of values such as the fundamental importance of empathic care must come from multiple contacts.

Social network scientists have done studies to determine how large a "stimulus crowd" is needed to get people walking down the street to look up at a high window on a building. When one person was staring up at the window, just 4 percent of passersby would stop and look up, but when 15 were staring up, 40 percent stopped to look. A stimulus crowd of just five produced almost as much effect as did much bigger groups.

The implication for healthcare organizations seeking to drive an epidemic of empathy is that highlighting individual role models may not be enough. Creating a critical mass of role models, getting clinicians together, and surrounding nonempathic clinicians with groups of empathic ones are all tactics that are likely to increase the effectiveness of spread of the desired value.

In fact, groups of clinicians often flip to better practice styles almost all at once. First, one or two clinicians start behaving in a different way, and others may or may not notice. But when three or four clinicians start behaving in the new way, most of the rest of the group will suddenly come along.

Rule 5: The Network Has a Life of Its Own

Christakis and his colleagues have shown that social networks have properties and functions that are not controlled or even perceived by the individuals within them; in other words, groups can be understood only as a whole. There is no one bird leading a flock of birds, but somehow they soar and dive and turn as a group. The researchers use the example of a cake, which has a taste that no single one of its components does. The whole is greater than the sum of its parts.

The question for healthcare organizations is this: How can we make our care seem to our patients more like a cake and less like the aisle in the grocery store with all the baking ingredients?

Mapping Social Networks in Healthcare

For social networks, function follows form. As Christakis notes, a pencil tip and a diamond are both composed of carbon, but their molecular structures determine whether they are soft and gray or hard and clear. The unique personality of a social network at any point in time is determined by the people in it and the types of connections among them. A network is built of nodes and connections.

The nodes are individuals. Although their genetics and acquired personality traits may determine how readily they form connections, their place in the network is determined by the number and strength of the connections they form.

The connections are the bonds between individuals. Reciprocal friendships form strong two-way bonds. One-way friendships form weak bonds. If you work in a large corporation with no middle management and your boss communicates by memo, he is likely to have hundreds of weak connections because few probably dare to write back to him. However, adding a layer of middle management whose feedback he values creates new stronger connections for the boss and adds more strong bonds between the managers and the workers they supervise. The workers are also likely to have a number of strong and weak bonds among one another that have sprung up for other reasons, such as working on projects together or sitting in the same pod.

Nodes with both strong and weak connections have a function and a value in a social network. People who form a lot of strong connections are likely to be near the center of a network, and they tend to form clusters with similar hubs. Those with weak connections are more likely to be at the periphery of the network. In that position they are well positioned to form bridges with other social networks, with which they may have stronger connections. Figure 5.1, which Christakis and Fowler created to illustrate the spread of

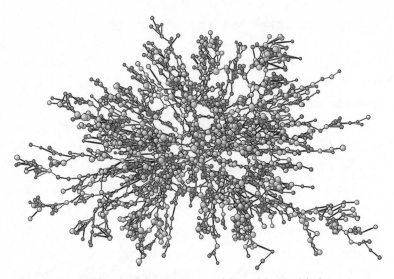

Figure 5.1   Largest connected subcomponent of the social network in the Framingham Heart Study in the year 2000. Reprinted from Nicholas A. Christakis and James H. Fowler, "The Spread of Obesity in a Large Social Network over 32 Years," *New England Journal of Medicine* 357, July 26, 2007: 370–379.

obesity through social networks, represents the connections among 2,200 people in the Framingham Heart Study.

Medical centers are rife with social networks that provide ideal structures for spreading values such as empathy, but those networks are not always apparent in the way one might imagine. The obvious networks of specialty divisions or service-worker unions may prove to be dead ends. Instead, the social networks with the greatest potential impact on the empathy and coordination of care are the teams that take care of patients, some of which are well defined, others of which are informal, and all of which are assembled differently for each individual patient.

How can you identify these social networks? Several software packages can be used to map all kinds of networks, but simple measures may suffice, as Christakis explained in the 2015 *Lancet* article referenced in note 11. In that study, Christakis and his colleagues recruited participants from three sets of nine villages in Honduras to receive nutritional supplements to hand out to their fellow villagers. In one set, the supplements were sent to random samples of villagers. In the second, they were sent to an equal number of villagers chosen because they had the strongest social ties. In the third, the researchers randomly identified the same number of villagers and asked them to name a friend, who then received the supplements to distribute.

The friends in the third village handed out 75 percent of the supplements, the randomly selected group in the first village delivered 66 percent, and the well-connected villagers in the second village delivered only 61 percent of the supplements they were given. This type of network targeting, without increasing the number of individuals targeted or the resources used, could be used to deliver all sorts of interventions, Christakis suggests.

In other words, simply ask a modest sample of clinical personnel who their friends are or who are the people they respect. See whose names come up more than once and you are on your way.

Tracking the Spread of Emotion

Just as collecting data from patients is the best way to measure whether patients' needs are being met, the best way to track the spread of emotions in a social network of healthcare personnel is to collect data from them. In most organizations, employee engagement data are collected only every year or two, but the clear trend is toward more frequent surveys. (It is easy to see that reporting very frequently on how things are going is likely to be part of the job for healthcare personnel in the future.)

The extreme version of data collection used in social network science is known as the experience-sampling method, which uses a series of alerts such as signals sent to a cell phone at varied (and thus unexpected) times, asking subjects to document their feelings, thoughts, and actions at that moment. For example, people may carry pocket devices and record moods four times per day over a five-day period. The data provide a detailed series of "emotional biopsies" from which a picture of the state of the social network can be defined.

From such data, researchers have been able to track the spread of emotions and values among teams of nurses and other groups of people working together, such as athletic teams. Data show that one positive person can improve the mood and performance of a group. Positive moods are associated with performance-enhancing changes, including more altruistic behavior, creativity, and efficient decision making.

Data show that there is a strong association between an athlete's happiness and the happiness of his or her teammates, and when a player's teammates are happier, performance improves. These findings naturally raise the question of whether happier healthcare providers might do a better job taking care of their patients. I'm not sure this is a question that requires a randomized controlled trial. There are plenty of data from employee engagement surveys that support the hypothesis that the mood and values of the social networks in a clinical workforce affect quality of care.

Emotions such as happiness are not quite the same thing as values, such as the sense that if I am not delivering empathic care to this patient, I will have trouble looking in the mirror later today. However, research on the way happiness spreads provides insight into how values can spread in a network. Indeed, one would expect values such as empathy to spread more quickly and reliably than emotions do, since they can be enforced through peer pressure.

Christakis and his colleagues have studied the question of whether happiness spreads just through dyads (i.e., between pairs of people) or whether there is also hyperdyadic spread: between you and your friends' friends, and their friends, and so on. They had previously found that the impact of changes such as obesity or changes in cigarette smoking habits fell off dramatically once one got beyond three degrees of separation.

When they mapped happiness among 1,020 people in the town of Framingham for whom they had detailed information on friends and other social relationships, there were two major findings. First, unhappy people tended to cluster with other unhappy people and happy people tended to cluster with other happy people. Second, unhappy people were more peripheral in social networks. They were much more likely to appear at the end of a chain of social relationships than in the middle.[12]

This kind of clustering could be the result of birds of a feather flocking together, but Christakis's research was able to show that there was also a causal effect of one person's happiness on another. Their analyses indicated that someone was about 15 percent more likely to be happy if she was directly connected to another person who was happy. At two degrees of separation, there was a 10 percent increased probability of being happy, and there was a 6 percent increase at three degrees. Beyond that, there was no measurable impact.

There is now a wealth of data examining various issues within the question of whether and how happiness spreads, whether distance in the relationships matters, and whether the transitivity of the social network matters. In short, these data indicate that emotions spread from person to person to person; in effect, they are contagious. However, emotions such as happiness do not sweep through a community and affect every person the way a plague can wipe out a town; the ripple effect peters out. For an epidemic of empathy to keep going, it must be driven from many different foci in an organization and constantly reinforced.

Social Isolation in Healthcare

The opposite of being connected is being unconnected, a lonely state that is all too common in modern medicine. As was detailed earlier, medical progress has led to both a massive increase in the number of people required to provide state-of-the-science care and a narrowing of their focus. Although there are many more people around, the irony is that the delivery of care is a lonelier experience than it was a generation ago.

For example, when I was an intern and resident at Peter Bent Brigham Hospital from 1979 to 1982, I felt that I knew everyone. It would take 20 minutes to walk 50 yards down the long hallway known as the Pike because I would run into friends and colleagues every few steps. During those interactions, we would discuss issues related to patients we shared and also plan to get together for dinner or the movies. We knew everything about everyone else's lives.

Once I was trying to read the newspaper before morning rounds, and another resident, a young woman who was trying to get pregnant, asked if I would cover her responsibilities in the emergency department for an hour during lunchtime. I had learned from a senior resident when I was an intern, "Never say no to a colleague, and there is a good chance that they will never say no to you." I did not even look up from the newspaper as I said, "Sure."

She continued standing there as I read the sports section. "Don't you want to know why?" she asked.

I put down the paper, smiled, and said, "I think I know." She told me anyway.

I bring this story up not to show what a generous colleague I am but to show what happens naturally in settings in which clinicians are thrown together, know that they are stuck together, and adopt a social norm such as "Never say no to a colleague." There were certainly some residents among us who did say no. Three decades later, my former cotrainees still talk about them, and we are a little cool to them when we see them at various events. When a critical mass of clinical personnel are connected as my coresidents were back then, good things happen, possibly including the births of the children of the resident whom I covered for that day.

I am sure there are still groups of friends in my hospital in which clinicians know one another as well as our group of residents did, but the fact is that healthcare has become a lonely life for many. Many outpatient physicians do not go to the hospital, and when they do, they do not recognize the clinicians who are taking care of their hospitalized patients. They may walk onto the floor of the hospital and no nurse or other doctor knows them by name.

The inpatient specialists have offices next to those of other clinicians with the same expertise, and they eat lunch in those offices—if there is time to eat. There is little time and opportunity for sitting in the cafeteria talking about cases, medical articles, or life itself. No one goes down to radiology to talk to the radiologists anymore. Lots of activity happens virtually and occurs much faster as a result, but the side effect is loneliness and social isolation.

For leaders hoping to drive an epidemic of empathy, this loneliness and social isolation should be seen for what it is: a major problem. Aside from the obvious challenge it poses for the spread of a value such as empathy, the fact is that isolated people are less happy and unhappy people are less able to feel and convey empathy.

Loneliness is a problem that feeds on itself. Research shows that people who feel lonely all the time lose friends faster than others do, are less likely to attract new friends, and are less able to name social connections. Loneliness can be epidemic in some organizations. Data suggest that being directly connected to someone who is lonely increases your risk of loneliness by 52 percent. At two degrees of separation, the risk increases 25 percent, and at three degrees of separation, the increase is 15 percent.[13]

Experienced researchers will have plenty of questions about what is cause and what is effect in these data, but experienced managers will recognize that there is a problem to be solved. That solution should begin by targeting people at the edges, to repair their social networks. It should also begin by spreading the connectedness of people who understand the meaning of "The Opposite of

Loneliness," the 2012 graduation speech given by the Yale senior Marina Keegan, who died in a car accident five days later, before she could begin her postgraduation job at *The New Yorker.*[14] She called it "this feeling that there are people, an abundance of people, who are in this together. Who are on your team." Her essay captured the sense of security and possibility that came with being a part of the social network of her graduating Yale class.

The Implications of Networks

The implications of the work of Burt, Christakis, and others in their field go well beyond the simple message that we all need to work more closely together, know one another better, and be nicer to patients. It would be naive to believe that the clock can be turned back to a simpler time when everyone knew everyone at a hospital. The to-do list for building social capital and driving an epidemic of empathy in medicine's modern era includes the following:

- Make the accumulation of social capital through brokerage and closure an important focus for leadership. Idea brokering should be as important an activity as any other type of research. Organizations should recognize that they need to build trust so that they can achieve closure on the best practices that create value for patients.

- Segment patients and providers into teams in which patients' needs can be better met through coordinated multi-disciplinary groups. Give those groups data on outcomes, including patient experience and costs. Concentrate patients on those teams so that there is critical mass. Colocate those teams and have them meet formally and informally.

- Identify the lonely and disconnected people in your network and try to bring them into the fold.

- Identify many of the positive and central influences in your network and put them together to create a persuasive powerful influence.

- Use an array of incentives—financial and others—to drive your epidemic of empathy, as is described in Chapter 6.

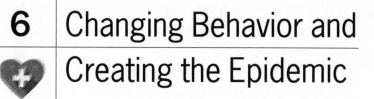

CHAPTER

6 Changing Behavior and Creating the Epidemic

WE KNOW THE problem: the chaos of modern medicine, which is a side effect of the marvelous progress in
our times. We can do so much more for patients than
we could a generation ago, but there has been an expo-
nential increase in the number of people involved in
delivering care even for routine issues. Those clinicians
often have narrow foci and overlook the big-picture
issues of greatest importance to patients. Frequently,
they are not working together as well as patients hope
and expect.

We have the imperative to improve. Healthcare providers are entering a marketplace driven by real competition on value. We have to deliver good outcomes
and meet patients' needs, including their psychological need for peace of mind, and do this as efficiently
as possible. Providing higher-value care is good for
patients and good for society and ultimately leads to
professional pride among healthcare personnel. That
pride makes coming to work more pleasant and leads
to lower turnover of personnel, which leads to better
business performance.

We know what we need to do. We understand the nature of empathy, and thanks to researchers such as Nicholas Christakis, we have the knowledge from social network science of how values such as empathetic care can spread.

The question is, How do we bring it all together? How do healthcare organizations and their leaders seize the competitive opportunity? How do we help individual clinicians live up to their aspirations to reliably deliver care that is safe, up to date, evidence-based, and efficient but also coordinated and compassionate?

Achieving reliable excellence is the essence of delivering healthcare—nothing more and nothing less. How do we do it for every patient every time? It's not really a change in behavior of healthcare providers that we seek. It is the achievement of consistency in being at our best.

Changing the Focus

Being reliably at our best in healthcare means doing something wonderful, remarkable, and uncontroversial, but the pursuit of consistency and the attempt to create the necessary teamwork can pose cultural issues. All too often, it seems that the strengths and weaknesses of healthcare are inextricably intertwined, creating a Gordian knot that defies unraveling. To visualize the resistance to redesigning care around the needs of patients, many healthcare leaders have to look in the mirror. That means people like me—doctors, mostly age 50 and older—who came into medicine in a different climate and different marketplace but are now in charge. Many of us still hold the belief that medicine is an art and a science but isn't a business, and most of us are resistant to change.

Nuanced Approach

One size will not fit all when it comes to driving improvement in healthcare. A nuanced, multidimensional approach is needed, because there are so many different people in healthcare and they are motivated on a day-to-day basis by different types of incentives. The truth is that we ourselves vary in the care we provide from hour to hour and patient to patient. This variability in healthcare personnel suggests that an epidemic of empathy cannot be driven solely through the use of the two major approaches employed by most healthcare organizations: carpet bombing and identifying bad apples.

In the carpet bombing approach, everyone is rallied to the organization's missions, often by being asked to watch videos, listen to speeches, take tests, and sometimes even take short courses on skills such as communication and listening. In the bad apple approach, the physicians and other personnel with the worst performance are taken aside, told they have a problem and must improve, and sometimes connected to coaches or courses to help them do so. If the bad apples cannot improve, they may be asked to leave the organization.

There are definitely important roles for carpet bombing and finding the bad apples, but driving an epidemic of empathy requires a more sophisticated approach than giving pep talks and playing Whac-A-Mole. In light of the forces that work against empathic care described in Chapter 1, these approaches are only going to slow deterioration, not accelerate improvement.

To drive improvement and make empathic care the norm, we need to use a range of tools, including financial and nonfinancial incentives, followed closely by giving clinicians help with the methods most likely to improve the care they provide. It doesn't take much to nudge clinicians in the right direction. After all, everyone in healthcare wants to deliver care that is compassionate and coordinated. However, although we are all humans—*good* humans—we are humans all the same. Left to our own devices, we are not as consistent as we would like to be both individually and collectively. We need incentives and nudges to be at our best and to try to improve.

Four Models for Social Action

The endlessly interesting question in patient experience pertains to how incentives for better healthcare performance should be designed. Should they be financial or nonfinancial? How can they be applied ethically and effectively?

In my 2014 article with Toby Cosgrove and an earlier essay with the ethicist Nikola Biller-Andorno,[1] I discussed an adaptation of the four models for social action described a century ago by the German economist and sociologist Max Weber:

1. **Tradition.** For example, a standard of behavior such as a dress code that if violated threatens one with expulsion from an institution

2. **Self-interest.** For example, the use of financial bonuses or penalties for achieving performance targets

3. **Affection.** For example, the use of peer pressure from one-on-one performance reviews or transparency with performance data

4. **Shared purpose.** For example, achievement of consensus that the overarching goal of a healthcare organization is to reduce the suffering of its patients

I will explore each of these four in detail, but the overall conclusion is that we need to use all four models in healthcare. Let's start with the creation of a shared purpose.

The vision that underlies a shared purpose—for example, Cleveland Clinic's Patients First or Mayo Clinic's constant reminders to its personnel for more than a century that "the needs of the patient come first"—comes from stories that capture what makes us proud or ashamed. Trying to deliver care with the elements that consistently bring pride to providers is what performance is all about, and no one can perform at a high level without first having a clear idea of what he or she is trying to achieve.

A shared purpose is necessary but not sufficient to drive a real epidemic of empathy. After all, tears dry and goose bumps subside. We need data and incentives to drive constant improvement and need to use the other three of Weber's levers to push clinicians to be at their best for every single patient. The reason we need to start with the creation of a shared purpose is the harsh reality that no measure is perfect and the data used to bring a measure to life will never be perfect either. Even if data are collected from every single patient, one can never be sure that all the risk factors that might bias the analysis in one direction or another have been taken into account.

If every measure has inherent weaknesses, if the data are unlikely to ever be complete, and if analyses cannot adjust for every risk factor, what can be done? Not measuring anything is obviously a bad idea. The implication is that we have to think clearly about what we are trying to do with the data and how we do it.

There are two very different questions one can ask when looking at performance data:

1. "Who is good enough?" or its variants, such as "Are we the best?" and "Am I good enough to have some credential, such as board certification, or to earn some financial incentive?"

2. "How can we get better than we currently are?" Here the question is how we can improve in the pursuit of a shared purpose. The assumption is that no matter how good we currently are, we should try to get better, and the data are a tool—albeit an imperfect one—to aid that progress.

Brent James of Intermountain Health has described this dichotomy, pointing out, "There are data for judgment, and there are data for improvement." When data are being used for improvement, they are intended for use for the second goal: trying to be better than we currently are.

The second question sounds nobler, of course, and one thing I have learned as life goes on is that when something sounds nobler, it usually is nobler. But the reality is that we need to address both questions. After all, organizations *do* have to decide whether to hire and fire people, and society *does* want to know whether a physician has achieved a certain level of mastery of his or her area of expertise as suggested by board certification.

Nevertheless, to drive an epidemic of empathy, healthcare organizations need to make a distinction between these two questions. The reason is that the two questions elicit very different responses from the personnel who are being evaluated. When data are being used for judgment, the issues have high stakes for the individuals involved, and the normal human response is to try to minimize the risk of failure. The best way to minimize that risk is to work hard to be as good as possible. But even for those who take that high road, an attractive backup plan is to attack the measures and the data that put one at risk for failure.

Attacking the measures can occur in several ways:

- **Focusing the measures on processes rather than actual patient outcomes.** The rationale for this approach is that many factors affect patients' actual outcomes, including how sick they are and whether they take their medications and adopt healthy lifestyles. In any business, the ultimate focus should be on the customer's outcome. But when the short-term focus is on passing judgment on clinicians, those clinicians want to be evaluated on the basis of processes within their control (e.g., prescribing a beta blocker for patients who have had a myocardial infarction). They also want those processes to be supported by evidence from rigorous research studies. The result is often a focus on process measures that do not differentiate among clinicians because everyone does them with a high rate of reliability.

- **Shifting accountability from the group to individuals.** Clinicians want to do a good job, but they see their jobs as individual efforts, not a team sport. They want feedback on issues for which they alone are responsible so that they can control their own fates. The problem with this perspective is that when many clinicians are involved in a patient's care, no one accepts full responsibility for improvement.

- **Identifying situations in which the measure could lead to unintended consequences.** For example, critics of measurement often hypothesize about what would happen if 100 percent compliance with the behavior supported by the measure were achieved and recall individual patients who might have been injured if such perfection had been the result of the use of a measure. They articulate fears that physicians might avoid caring for the sickest patients or ignore patients who are not the focus of the measures. For example, they might contend that diabetes measures could cause physicians to ignore nondiabetics.

After poking holes in the measures, clinicians who are unhappy with performance measurement turn to the data used to bring measures to life. Again, the reality is that the data and the analyses are never perfect and cannot be used to prove most issues beyond a shadow of reasonable doubt. The data are rarely complete; for example, patient experience surveys tend to be completed by only about 20 percent of patients. Patients cannot be compelled to complete surveys, and there is always speculation about the differences between those who do and those who don't.

Even if 100 percent of patients completed surveys, populations of patients vary in ways that affect the outcome. It is possible to adjust for some of the factors that influence patient experience and other outcomes, but it is impossible to know if every important difference in populations has been taken into account. Of course, collecting and managing the data needed for risk adjustment requires work and time. The bottom line: in my long management career, I have spent many hours and dollars on risk adjustment, but I don't think I have made anyone happy—less angry, perhaps, but not happy.

A New Measurement Goal

But what if the goal of measurement is improvement in the pursuit of a noble shared purpose rather than punishment? In that case, many of the issues discussed above are viewed in a different light if not dismissed altogether. If the real goal is to be better next year than you are now, risk adjustment is not a stumbling block, assuming that your patient population is not changing in a major way. You are comparing yourself to yourself; no risk adjustment is needed.

The data sampling may be far from complete, but if there is no systematic difference in the way patients are identified and contacted, the populations are likely to be similar. Someone has to prove that they are different before anyone can blame changes (or lack of change) on differences in the population.

Measures may have inherent potential flaws, but if the goal is improvement, it is clear that *not* measuring is a terrible strategy. I like to remind physicians that we have to make decisions for patients with imperfect data all the time. There are some physicians who are paralyzed by uncertainty and cannot make a decision without ordering one more test, then another test after that, and so on. We know that uncertainty will always be with us and that the physicians who cannot act because of it are not the doctors we ourselves want to go to.

The same is true for improvement of healthcare delivery. The measures and data will never be perfect. We should make them as complete and as good as we can, but at a certain point, if the goal is improvement, we have to use the data that are available and try to get better.

When the goal is improvement rather than judgment, providers can use measures for which 100 percent is not the ideal target. In fact, measures—and the variation that they reveal—are most interesting and have the most impact when they capture the tension between two competing values. For example, when surgeons decide whether to operate on a very sick patient, they have to weigh short-term risks (the chances that the operation might cause the patient to die or have other immediate complications) against the potential long-term benefits (the chances that the patient will live a longer or healthier life because of the operation).

It is obvious that you don't want to choose a cardiac surgeon with a mortality rate of 100 percent. It is less obvious that you probably don't want a cardiac surgeon who has a mortality rate of zero—no patient ever dies—because that surgeon is probably emphasizing short-term safety over long-term outcome. That risk-averse surgeon may be declining to operate on patients who have a high risk of complications with surgery but who have an even greater risk of dying without the operation. The best surgical mortality rate might be somewhere close to the middle of the pack.

Here is an analogous example: Among patients with pain, it is obviously not a good idea to give narcotics to every patient, but it is also a bad idea to never give patients narcotics. If a clinician learns that his or her prescribing habits or his or her patients' reports of pain control are vastly different from those of other clinicians, that clinician might have something to learn from colleagues.

For clinicians to perform well enough to meet some minimal standard, measures and data must sometimes be used for judgment. However, to drive improvement so that organizations can respond to competition, clinicians must have a different perspective. They have to believe that the goal is improvement. And the only way that they will give their all to the goal of improvement is if they share a noble purpose.

The Importance of Shared Purpose

Clinicians are willing to act on imperfect data and use measures for which 100 percent is not the ideal target when there is a compelling goal, such as the care of a patient. For healthcare organizations, there needs to be a similarly compelling shared purpose to put performance measures and data in perspective. If there is a goal for an organization that is as compelling as saving a patient's life, personnel are unlikely to get stuck reviewing measures and data for reasons not to believe their implications. Instead, they will assess the best data available to them and try to get better.

That is why when one is considering the four models for social action from the work of Max Weber, the first that should be addressed is shared purpose. Shared purpose is different from the other models in that it is created through narrative, not data. It is developed through the stories that cause providers to feel pride or shame. These stories can be deconstructed, and the factors that provide intrinsic motivation to clinicians can be identified. Measures and data can then be used—despite their imperfections—via Weber's other models for social action in pursuit of this shared purpose.

How does an organization develop a shared purpose? As Toby Cosgrove and I wrote in our 2014 *Harvard Business Review* article, the creation of shared purpose begins with the same steps used to build consensus in any organization: listening, demonstrating respect for different views, and creating processes through which everyone can be heard and contribute. However, healthcare has special challenges: the diversity of types of work to be done, the training of the personnel, and the organizational structures within which they work (e.g., employed versus affiliated physicians). Shared purpose has to transcend all the factors that divide provider personnel; after all, that's what being shared is about.

These discussions have to acknowledge that we have a natural tendency to dwell on our problems, such as rising costs, lack of access, and disappointing quality. We don't give much time or energy to what we are trying to create or the possibility of a better future. But to help our colleagues move beyond grief and anger about what they might be losing as their organizations respond to the market's imperatives for quality and efficiency, leaders have to shift the conversation to something different: something positive, something noble, something that transcends the concerns of any of us as individuals.

Only one goal meets those criteria: improving care for patients, which means meeting their needs and improving their outcomes. That focus has to be the core of any change agenda that demands sacrifice from clinicians.

At the same time, leaders must acknowledge the need for sacrifices. Individual clinicians will lose some personal autonomy as they work in effective teams, and that may or may not be offset by an increase in the group's autonomy. There may well be losses of income. No leader should make promises that the status quo will be preserved and expect to have more than a few years before those words come back to haunt him or her. No leader should say that the organization will prioritize doctors' interests over those of patients. Instead, leaders should emphasize that the journey will be difficult but the goal of high-value care is central to the professional pride of the organization as well as business viability.

Skeptical readers may question whether clinical personnel are too jaded by modern times to respond to lofty visions. I think that the opposite is true and that nurses and physicians in particular are driven by intrinsic motivations. The most vivid examples occur during catastrophes. During Hurricane Sandy and the Boston Marathon bombings, no doctors or nurses worried about compensation. In fact, the clinical personnel who were unable to get involved and directly contribute in some way were disappointed. They knew that they had missed out on something good, one of the rewards of being in medicine that transcend money.

What about when the catastrophe is longer term, playing out over years or more? Healthcare personnel can still rise to the occasion. One of my favorite examples is the campaign to save Grady Health System in Atlanta, which was losing millions weekly and was on the verge of bankruptcy for at least half of the decade 2000–2010. The question being asked about Grady, along with other safety-net hospitals around the country, was often not whether it would collapse but when and how and what would happen next.

Leaders from Grady and local government conceived a brilliant campaign with the tagline "Atlanta Can't Live Without Grady." One of its leaders, Matt Gove, told me how that campaign grew out of the need to communicate what was obvious to anyone who walked the halls of Grady or the streets around it: it would be a disaster for hundreds of thousands of people if Grady further deteriorated or closed.

The campaign started simply with photos of patients or prominent Atlantans with the Grady logo over their hearts under the "Atlanta Can't Live Without Grady" tagline. Over time, the campaign evolved to include detailed and moving stories of people who were saved at Grady, each one with the quote "I Wouldn't Be Here Without Grady."

Can an organization be rescued by inspiration? A lot of other types of work were going on at the same time, of course, and help came from the outside, in part because of the campaign. Grady received more than $300 million in philanthropic commitments, and the state passed a hospital-provider fee that helped support institutions like Grady that serve large numbers of Medicaid patients. Clearly, foundations and politicians got the message that Atlanta couldn't live without Grady.

Working a thousand miles to the north in Boston, I heard about the Grady campaign because I learned that it changed the culture of the hospital, that morale improved and personnel turnover declined. Again, many factors surely played a role besides the articulation of a shared vision of what Grady meant to Atlanta. But the fact is that Grady is still there, and I am sure the campaign had something to do with it. The relevant question at many safety-net institutions is not whether an organization can be rescued by inspiration; it's whether an organization can be rescued without it.

Adding "Shared" to the Purpose

One basic problem that healthcare leaders often describe in creating a sense of shared purpose is the "shared" part. Physicians in particular, they say, don't want to work in teams. They don't see themselves as part of an organization even if they are employees of a hospital or healthcare system or their own physician group. There is a fantasy among some that employed doctors follow orders. Anyone who has worked in an organization with employed doctors knows that they are doctors first and employees second—a *distant* second.

As doctors, they view their duty to patients as preempting other obligations. This next statement is a broad generalization to which some exceptions can probably be readily identified, but here goes: my strong belief is that the vast majority of physicians won't do things that they know are counter to their patients' interests no matter how great the financial incentives are. I am not naive; if financial incentives nudge them in that direction, physicians may talk themselves into believing that some tests or treatments might be beneficial for patients even if the evidence is thin, even lame. But their ego identity as advocates for patients is a more powerful force than financial incentives in many settings. Major financial incentives to do things that have no connection to meeting patients' needs tend to have mixed effectiveness at best, but it takes only modest incentives to nudge clinicians to do something that they know to be the right thing for patients. Often it takes no financial incentive at all.

The implication of this dynamic is that doctors' and nurses' intrinsic motivations provide a path to meaningful change. The leaders of healthcare organizations can engage their personnel by putting the focus on patients and their suffering, which every clinician agrees trumps all other concerns on a short-term basis. The goal is to make that prioritization endure, for every patient, on the weekends as well as the weekdays, in the middle of the night, throughout the year.

The creation of a shared purpose begins with stories, not data. These are the stories that crystallize how providers want to see themselves. They are the cases that bring providers pride or bring them shame. Accordingly, discussions with clinicians about reorganizing care should never begin with talk of contracts and compensation or numerical trends in issues that seem related to excellent patient care only indirectly. For example, waiting time for patients is an important business issue for every healthcare organization and a major source of annoyance and anxiety to patients. But clinicians tend to think of that issue as something that is not as important as doing as good a job with the patient right in front of them and do not readily see how that complex issue is under their control.

Sometimes a single case is sufficient to galvanize clinicians. In 2008, a patient called Cleveland Clinic's urology department and asked for an appointment. His problem was difficulty urinating, and he was given the next available appointment, which was two weeks away. That evening, he was in the emergency department because he could not urinate at all. The patient was not permanently harmed, but he certainly experienced several hours of exquisite discomfort.

Cleveland Clinic's leaders discussed the case, and one of them asked, "Do we want to be the type of organization that doesn't even *try* to figure out if patients should be seen right away?" With that perspective and with the embarrassment resulting from one case, they decided that their current appointment system was intolerable and they had to try to do better. Cleveland Clinic ultimately introduced a same-day appointment policy in which every patient who calls for an appointment is asked if he or she would like to be seen that day. If patients do, they may have to drive an hour to an available clinician, but they are almost always seen. Cleveland Clinic now handles about 1 million of its 5.5 million annual patient visits on the same day, and this policy has helped the clinic expand its market share. It was not a marketing executive's brainchild; it came from clinicians' resolve to do better over a single case.

To engage clinicians and other personnel, statements of shared purpose must be simple and direct. An example that I admire is Cleveland Clinic's simple statement "Patients First." Distributing 40,000 lapel buttons with those two words was one of the first acts by Toby Cosgrove when he became CEO in 2004. Many other organizations had considered that kind of statement before and since and struggled with the implications ("Doctors Second"). But addressing rather than ignoring the implications is the reason such a shared purpose is so critical to business success.

After all, one of the key lessons about strategy described in Chapter 2 is that organizations have to have clarity on their definition of success. They have to know the goal. A mission statement that reflects multiple purposes, all of which are noble (research, teaching, and patient care is the classic three-part mission for academic medical centers), sounds good but does not provide a framework for guiding tough decisions. Organizations that want to survive and thrive in a healthcare market driven by competition on value have to make decisions.

As forward-looking organizations recognize the need to make choices and articulate a clear top priority, the needs of patients always come first. It is a dynamic that makes me proud to be in healthcare, in which we have lots of good people who want to do good things for patients. That dynamic also happens to be good business thinking: meeting the needs of patients as well and as efficiently as possible (i.e., value) is the one goal that every stakeholder in healthcare supports.

For more than a century, the Mayo Clinic has promised that "the needs of the patient come first." Like most great healthcare organizations, Mayo has a long, complicated mission and values statement, but that phrase about the needs of patients (uttered long ago by one of the founding Mayo brothers) is considered the primary value.

Mayo clinicians do more than mouth this phrase. They have differentiating patterns of care, such as the expectation that the first specialist to see patients will continue to follow them even when the focus of care has drifted into another area. For example, if a patient referred to a heart failure specialist turns out to have lung disease, that patient is connected to a pulmonary specialist, but the first doctor continues to follow the patient and makes sure all the care is coordinated. It's obviously better for patients, but this kind of coordination occurs only by accident at most academic medical centers.

When I ask Mayo clinicians why they are willing to do what their counterparts elsewhere will not, I always get the same answer: "Well, here at Mayo, the needs of the patient come first, and. . . ." They don't roll their eyes when they repeat what might seem a platitude in other settings. They say it with the same matter-of-factness with which they say, "It gets really cold here in the winter."

Intermountain Healthcare in Utah adopted a new, short, and direct mission statement in 2014: "Helping people live the healthiest lives possible." This replaced their prior mission statement, which was "Excellence in the provision of healthcare to the communities in the Intermountain West." Note the shift in focus from reliability in what providers do to the more challenging, nebulous, but aspirational goal of meeting the needs of patients.

These and other effective statements of shared purpose have key features in common. First, they are unequivocally focused on patients. Second, they describe an aspirational goal—meeting patients' needs—that will never be completely achieved. Improvement will always be possible and an imperative. Part of the subtext of these shared purposes is that hard work will not be enough; it will take greater group effectiveness to make progress.

Appreciative Inquiry

A valuable tool for fleshing out shared purpose is appreciative inquiry: focusing on the positive, identifying the cases that make caregivers proud, and trying to make the key elements of great care happen reliably instead of by chance. Cleveland Clinic makes every employee spend half a day in appreciative inquiry exercises with other staff members. Hennepin County Medical Center in Minneapolis has had "patient rallies" in which staff members sit with patients to discuss cases in which care has been excellent.

At the hospital where I practice, Brigham and Women's Hospital in Boston, the emergency department began a multi-year journey that took its overall patient experience ratings from the sixth percentile to the ninety-ninth percentile by discarding its negative patient comments and focusing on the positive ones. The messages in the positive comments were the flip side of the negative ones. Patients appreciated when they were seen promptly and treated with respect and when coordination of care with their other clinicians was excellent. These positive comments shaped the Brigham emergency department's overall goal: "VIP care for all."

Of course, the emergency department needed much more than a slogan. It received more space from the hospital to expand its capacity. Department leaders created even more space by using lean management techniques, through which they concluded that the triage function was using space and personnel that could be better employed in direct patient care. And they deployed a range of financial and nonfinancial incentives to reward VIP care for all. The result was improvement in patient experience to the very top tiers of emergency medicine.[2]

The work began with the articulation of a shared purpose. It put the complex choices that had to follow in perspective and made clear which goal should be prioritized when there were difficult decisions to be made.

Financial Incentives

Financial incentives certainly catch people's attention. After all, almost everyone is motivated in part by financial incentives and job security. Even if their organization's shared purpose resonates deeply with them, people sit up and pay attention to whatever measures are being used to assess their performance. They want to know what data are available for those measures and how the data are analyzed. This interest is intensified tremendously if financial incentives are based on those measures.

The attention that results from financial incentives can do both good and harm. As has been noted, financial incentives draw attention to topics that might otherwise be ignored. However, when data are used for judgment—loss of a financial incentive qualifies as an adverse judgment outcome—the natural response is to try to reduce the risk of loss for that incentive, make the targets as easy to attain as possible, and raise concern about the quality of the data and the analyses.

There is no single right way to use financial incentives, but there are certainly some mistakes to be avoided. Some organizations make portions of clinicians' compensation dependent on patient experience performance and are still struggling to find the best way to do it. Pennsylvania-based Geisinger Health System ties 20 percent of physicians' compensation to their performance against certain goals, but improved patient experience ratings account for a very small portion of their performance-related income.[3] Many other organizations are attaching 1 or 2 percent or more of clinicians' income to improvement in patient experience scores. Some are basing incentive awards on reaching a minimum threshold, such as ranking in the seventy-fifth percentile of measures of physician performance for the group or for individual physicians.

This approach definitely gets patient experience on clinicians' radar screens, but problems with financial incentives are intertwined with their strengths. People really hate to lose money. Prospect theory, one of the core concepts in behavioral economics, explains why. Prospect theory asserts two major themes, the first of which is that proportion matters: If you give people $100, they are happy. If you give them $200, they are happier, but they are not twice as happy. The second major theme is that losses affect people more than gains do. If someone gives you $100, you are happy, but you may forget to mention it when you get home for dinner that night. But if you lose $100, perhaps because you got a speeding ticket, you may be in a bad mood for the rest of the day.

The powerful message from prospect theory is that small packets of incentive dollars that are framed as potential losses provide the most return on the incentive dollar. If clinicians realize that failure to achieve a performance goal will lead to a loss of just 1 percent of their income, they will work hard to avoid that loss, especially if the performance goal is consistent with their notion of delivering excellent care. They hate the idea of losing a small incentive because of failure to do something they really ought to do. As a result, they may work long and hard to get it, even if means *not* doing things that might *increase* their income by 2 percent.

The dark side of financial incentives is intertwined with their strengths. When clinicians lose their financial incentive, they are deeply unhappy. They focus on the flaws in the measures, data, and analyses and demand an appeals process that can consume more resources than are actually at stake. Those dynamics are familiar to every leader who has used financial incentives to try to drive improvement in patient experience, and they should be recognized as the expected result of normal human behavior.

Financial incentives that are attached to getting to a specific percentile for individual or groups of physicians are particularly problematic. The intentions of such targets are noble. The leadership and governance of the organization may decide that they do not want to be just okay; they want to be outstanding. Therefore, they set a target such as the seventy-fifth or ninetieth percentile for overall physician performance.

Those targets may simply not be feasible for some groups or individuals with a high proportion of patients, such as Asians or New Yorkers, who tend to give lower ratings. Financial incentives for quality also tend to create a floor but do not provide a motivation for pushing beyond what is needed to avoid the pain of missing the target. That dynamic is particularly problematic if the floor has been negotiated down to something that everyone can easily reach. Therefore, financial incentives for quality often are associated with one of two unattractive outcomes: they fail to motivate outstanding performance, or they infuriate large numbers of personnel who fall short of the target. Sometimes they do both.

Because of such issues, many organizations use financial incentives for improvement in patient experience as a transition tactic. Modest incentives draw clinicians' attention to patient experience, and then the organization transitions to the nonfinancial tactics described below.

Nonfinancial Incentives: Increased Affection and Respect

Some organizations, such as Cleveland Clinic, Kaiser Permanente, and many academic medical centers, have avoided financial incentives and emphasized Max Weber's affection model for social action, using peer pressure and the desire for respect to drive improvement. At Cleveland Clinic, for example, every physician is on a one-year contract and doctors undergo rigorous annual performance reviews. Intense feedback, including patient experience, is used to create accountability for performance and improvement in all areas. At other organizations, a mixed model is emerging in which financial incentives are being used for issues with very direct financial implications, such as the volume of services or the efficiency of care, and nonfinancial incentives are employed to improve the quality of care.

In fact, nonfinancial incentives are emerging as the preferred approach for issues that are predominantly related to the quality of care. No one wants to lose the respect of his or her colleagues, family, or friends. We all have egos to protect. This approach seems particularly appropriate to patient experience, in which no clinicians should be calculating whether they would be better off financially if they mustered the energy to demonstrate empathy to a patient. The decision should be based on the adoption of social norms. It should be a "can I look at myself in the mirror?" decision.

Transparency as Incentive

The fear of loss of affection and respect explains why many organizations have been successful in driving improvement without financial incentives. Some, such as Cleveland Clinic, use intense one-on-one annual performance reviews. An increasing number of institutions are ramping up the pressure through internal transparency, letting all of a clinician's colleagues see his or her data, including patient comments.

Transparency, even when only one's colleagues are seeing the data, is uncomfortable. That discomfort is essential for driving improvement, but clinical leaders have to find a middle ground in which they are pushing the organization ahead but not provoking open rebellion. That said, it is critical that provider leaders recognize when they are shying away from creating real pressure. Here are some potential warning signs that organizations may not be taking full advantage of the power of the affection model:

- **Blinding.** Some organizations share data but do not reveal the names of individual physicians.

- **Chaos.** Others may reveal the names but do not organize the comments by physician, making it hard for anyone to draw conclusions about any individual's performance.

- **No analysis.** Many avoid rank ordering data, making it hard to discern who is doing well and who is not, thus softening the blow for those who may be well below average.

- **Rose-colored glasses.** Some share only positive comments.

The big breakthrough in the use of transparency to drive improvement in patient experience was created by the University of Utah Health Care, which was the first to make systematic full transparency of patient experience data part of its approach to improvement. The University of Utah's leadership made this bold leap in the winter of 2012–2013 after a three-year journey that began with the decision to move from using mail or telephone surveys of a sample to employing electronic surveys of as many patients as possible. After they began feeding much more data and comments back to their physicians, they moved to internal transparency. After two years of viewing one another's data, they decided to let the rest of the world see them as well.

The improvement achieved at University of Utah was startling. It went from having 1 percent of its physicians in the top 1 percent of Press Ganey's overall physician ratings (exactly what would be expected) to 15 percent with internal transparency and to more than 25 percent of physicians in the exclusive group with public transparency. No organization that I know of has ever achieved anything like this kind of improvement with any financial incentive. University of Utah Health Care made this startling progress without putting a single dollar on the line for any of its physicians. It was all due to Weber's affection lever.

Although transparency is a bit unnerving to clinicians, movement in this direction is accelerating in part because of the proliferation of online consumer review websites. A 2013 Pew Research Center study determined that 72 percent of adult Internet users had searched online for information about health issues in the previous 12 months.[4] A study in the *Journal of the American Medical Association* reported that 59 percent of American adults strongly consider online ratings when choosing a physician. Over one-third of individuals using online reviews chose their physicians on the basis of positive reviews, and 37 percent avoided doctors with negative reviews.[5]

Clinicians are not happy with the information available on many of these sites, which generally require that patients take the initiative to log on and enter a review, as opposed to reviews stimulated by a patient's response to a prompt delivered by e-mail or another type of communication. The numbers of surveys or comments used to profile physicians on many sites are often extremely small, and the sites assign "star ratings" that are based on as few as two or three reviews. In addition, the proportion of negative reviews tends to be higher when patients have to take the initiative to provide information, presumably because unhappy patients are more likely to act than are patients who have had the good experiences they expected.

In addition, there is no guarantee that the information actually comes from patients who saw that physician or visited that facility. Researchers from MIT and Northwestern University examined 325,869 online consumer reviews and found that almost 5 percent were submitted by customers with no confirmed transaction. Those questionable reviews also included a significantly higher proportion of negative comments.[6]

When an organization works hard to get e-mail addresses and surveys are sent electronically to all patients by e-mail, the number of responses per clinician goes up dramatically. That has the happy effect of moving provider find-a-doctor websites to the top of the page on search engines. The reason is that search engines prioritize sites with more and fresher data. Thus, the constant influx of new comments to provider-driven transparency sites is rewarded with more attention, as it should be.

Before Utah began publishing online reviews, its physician profile page views totaled 32,144 per month. Three months after implementation, monthly page views increased nearly fourfold to 122,072. Piedmont Health had similar results with a 200 to 300 percent increase in web traffic. Both organizations' find-a-doctor websites display significantly more reviews than any third-party review site, and there has been a marked increase in their visibility in search results.

It has not taken long for Utah's example to spread. Within two years, Wake Forest and Piedmont had rolled out their own programs, and Stanford followed shortly thereafter. When you talk to colleagues at University of Utah and other places that have gone down this path, you learn that transparency changes the way physicians look at each patient encounter. They recognize that each interaction is high stakes for both the patient and themselves. The patient has a high probability of being surveyed, and he or she may write a negative comment, but in fact, the patient is about 10 times as likely to write a positive one.

The focus of transparency is not on any individual metric. It is on trying to take better care of patients and feeling real pressure to do so for every single one of them. The pressure is relentless, but it is pressure to be the kind of clinicians that we want to think of ourselves as being. I haven't met a physician or nurse yet who thinks this kind of pressure is perverse.

Using the Tradition Lever

People working in healthcare ought to be proud of what they do and where they work. They should be motivated by that pride, and they should worry about the implications of deviating so markedly from the norms of the organization that they are asked to leave. No one wants to lose his or her income, of course, but there are important nonfinancial losses as well: the prestige, security, and sense of self-worth that come with being part of a respected organization.

One of my favorite examples of tradition in action is the Mayo Way, which characterizes the approach to a wide range of activities of the Mayo Clinic not just at its mother ship in Rochester, Minnesota, but throughout its system. For example, as was described in Chapter 5, there is a clear expectation that clinicians will answer their pagers immediately. They don't finish their conversations. They don't finish their e-mails. They don't finish their television shows or movies. They answer at once.

I learned about this social norm from a leader of radiology at Mayo's facility in Arizona. She told me that her radiologists tend not to recommend additional testing at the end of their interpretations of tests. Instead, they simply page the physicians who are directly involved in the patients' care and discuss what to do next. The radiologists are willing to do this because they know they can get a response from the other clinicians right away. It makes the radiologists feel more like they are part of a team taking care of patients as opposed to being technologists sitting in a dark room working their way down a long list of images. I can't prove that this pattern of care is better or more efficient, but I'd be shocked if that was not the case.

When I learned of this cultural standard at Mayo Clinic, I began asking physicians there, "What happens if you don't answer right away?" Some looked genuinely puzzled, as if I had suggested truly deviant behavior. One said, "Well, you won't do well here." Another said, "The last thing you want is for people to say, 'He's the kind of guy who doesn't answer his page right away.'"

There are other aspects of the Mayo Way, of course, including the expectation that the first physician who sees a patient will take care of that patient even if the patient's issues turn out to fall outside that physician's area of expertise. There is also a dress code. The message is clear: "There is a Mayo way of doing things. Don't come here if you don't want to adopt it—completely." The standards translate into high-quality, well-coordinated care that is a source of pride throughout the Rochester area and that patients willingly travel long distances to access.

To use the tradition lever, organizations must be ready to part company with personnel who are unwilling or unable to adhere to the norms and work with their colleagues toward their shared purpose. In the past, hospitals often welcomed almost any decent physician who would bring patients and therefore revenue to the institution. Physicians rarely lost their credentials or were fired. That still does not happen often, but when it does, colleagues usually ask, "What took so long?"

Providing Examples

Max Weber's models provide motivation to drive an epidemic of empathy, but clinicians also need examples, as was described in Chapter 5. The bad apple approach is not enough; clinicians need to be able to learn from their colleagues who have developed empathic care patterns over the years and made certain actions routine in their practices.

The apprenticeship approach still has its place in medicine, and the level of detail at which learning occurs can be quite minute. For example, I have made some questions I learned from admired colleagues part of my routine patient care visits. I had one of my patients come back from a consultation with the cardiologist Dale Adler and say how impressed he was when Dale said, "Tell me what your life is like." Now I ask that of virtually every patient, knowing that the open-ended format allows patients to talk about what is most important to them while giving me information about their physical and psychological status.

Similarly, from my own primary care physician, Charles Morris, MD, I learned to say to patients, "Help me understand what I can do to help you." I use that near the end of almost all complicated visits both to get patients' hopes right out on the table and to make clear that I consider it my job to help them.

I learned those two questions by accident, but many organizations aren't relying on chance encounters between clinicians. They are taking steps to celebrate clinical champions and spread their best practices systematically. They are having large-scale meetings at which physicians and nurses share their tips and assigning individual clinicians to work directly with such champions in some cases. These steps send the message that empathic care is important to the organization but also that it is possible and that it does not conflict with overall clinical excellence. In fact, empathic care is at the core of clinical excellence.

One valuable lesson from the social network research of Christakis and others is that the impact of these positive examples can be augmented if they are concentrated and presented in a group. That grouping transmits the message that the organization is not just focusing on one exceptional individual but that a norm is in development. As was described in Chapter 5, groups tend to tip when a critical mass (e.g., three or four clinicians) has adopted a new and better way of delivering care.

Providing the Tools

There is still work to be done even after motivating clinicians to provide more empathic care and giving them models. For example, communication skills come naturally to some but not all clinicians. Some organizations are requiring that all clinicians undergo training in communication with patients. At the very least, training should be made available to those for whom patient data suggest substantial opportunities to improve. Another way to identify clinicians for whom such training would be useful is to have trained observers sit in on a sample of patient interactions.

An outstanding description of the tools that have proved most useful to providers can be found in the book *Service Fanatics* by my colleague James Merlino, MD, the former chief experience officer at Cleveland Clinic. This book not only describes tools such as communication training in detail but also places them in the context of the journey of an organization from disappointing to excellent performance. A deeper and valuable description of that communication training program can be found in the book by two of Merlino's former physician colleagues at Cleveland Clinic, Adrienne Boissy and Timothy Gilligan, *Communication the Cleveland Clinic Way: How to Drive a Relationship-Centered Strategy for Exceptional Patient Experience.*

The Role of Governing Boards

Using any of Weber's four levers is challenging and disruptive to frontline healthcare providers. These approaches are the kinds of measures that sound better when they are part of a speech, article, or book than they do when you are a busy clinician trying to get through your day. For that reason, the very good people in healthcare often push back on steps that will improve it.

Great healthcare organizations tend to have great leaders and great boards behind those leaders. They have directors/trustees/ overseers who understand the meaning of strategy, who remind management to focus not just on the rocks in the water but on the horizon as well. They track metrics that reflect progress toward goals and help management through the tough choices that must be made when change is the imperative.

Around the country, boards of forward-looking healthcare organizations are adapting to the challenges of the new era. Here are a few noteworthy examples:

- Some organizations start board meetings with the presentation of an actual patient case, often one in which the outcome was poor. Sometimes the patient is brought into the room to drive home the message that the issue under discussion has had a real impact on a real human being. The board and management discuss what went wrong and why and review what is being done to reduce the chances that the patient's adverse outcome will ever happen again.

- Many boards are devoting part of every meeting's agenda to reviewing quality data, often deliberately placing this agenda item before financial reports so that time is available and energy is high when quality data are being discussed. This reverses a traditional dynamic of putting quality data after financial discussions and often running out of time for topics such as patient experience and safety.

- Some boards have quality committees that meet with senior management to review performance so that data can be explored in greater depth than is possible at a meeting of the full board. These committees are considered the counterparts of board finance committees.

- Some boards are making sustained explicit efforts to get members out of their chairs and into patient care settings. University of Utah Health Care's board assigns each member to a patient-care unit. Board members visit the unit monthly, meeting staff and interviewing patients. Utah also has had board members go through an exercise in which they were told they had a disease (e.g., heart failure) and had to search for information and explore decisions that a patient with that condition would have to make.

Holding management accountable is impossible without good data and in ample amounts. That means a measurement/analytic/accountability strategy that goes beyond small samples of patients. Organizations need enough data so that worrisome trends cannot be dismissed as meaningless and individual patient-care units and clinicians themselves can feel the pressure to improve and identify role models. The data will never be perfect, but boards should not allow management to be paralyzed by the inevitable imperfections. After all, paralysis is the worst possible strategy for any healthcare organization.

Boards should be looking at an array of quality data that include but also go beyond patient experience at every meeting, including the following:

- **Mortality.** Expected versus observed mortality is readily calculated for the overall patient population and for specific conditions that are the focus of government value-based purchasing programs (acute myocardial infarction, pneumonia, and heart failure). Boards should place mortality data in perspective, however, and know that they are important yet are not the sole relevant measure of quality. It is not realistic to expect providers to be statistically better than expected for mortality, as the biggest determinant of mortality is the burden of disease in individual patients. However, if mortality is worse than expected, it should be considered an organizational crisis.

- **Clinical metrics that are the focus of value-based purchasing initiatives.** Examples include readmission rates for acute myocardial infarction, heart failure, pneumonia, chronic obstructive lung disease, and major total joint replacement. These metrics are, of course, important to patients with these conditions and are increasingly available publicly. They therefore help shape the organization's brand. More important, board focus on these measures encourages management to organize teams that can improve these condition-specific outcomes.

- **Metrics that are drivers of market share, such as patient experience data.** These metrics are the most direct measure of the organization's overall effectiveness in meeting patients' needs and giving them peace of mind that their clinicians are working well together on their behalf. Analyses in every patient setting—inpatient, outpatient, emergency department, and so on—show that what patients value most are the competency, empathy, and communication skills of clinicians and the coordination of care. Patients are not that interested in amenities such as food and parking, and boards should not be distracted by them either.

- **Measures of effectiveness of care for condition-specific subsets.** An example would be patient reported outcome measures (PROMs). These measures are different from the process measures that are used in value-based purchasing initiatives, as they cannot be calculated by analyzing insurance claims; they require asking patients about their outcomes and whether their needs have been met. Relatively few organizations collect such data yet, but boards should encourage management to move down this path because hospitals and physician groups are important but limited units of analysis and improvement. When subsets of patients with similar shared needs can be identified and teams can be organized to meet those needs, major gains in effectiveness and efficiency can be achieved. These teams need data to guide their efforts to improve, and only patients can provide information on the outcomes that matter to them. Boards should not allow management to assert that their organizations are delivering world-class care without measuring actual outcomes.

- **Engagement of clinicians and other employees.** Organizations need a workforce that takes pride in delivering excellent care and doing so as efficiently as possible. Organizations with better engagement data have lower turnover rates and better financial and quality performance.

With the right governance, the right leadership, and the right management, healthcare organizations can achieve clarity on their goals, use incentives wisely, and drive an epidemic of empathy.

7 Ten Key Steps
Toward Higher-Value Empathic Healthcare

RECOGNIZING THE INFORMATION overload we all face today and the many mandates, strategic imperatives, and recommendations that compete for top priority among providers of healthcare, here are 10 key steps that I hope will be useful in creating the context for and driving an epidemic of empathy in healthcare. I will start by being broad and strategic and get specific and tactical as the list goes on. The perspective may seem optimistic, but I believe the steps are grounded in reality and are consistent with the basic values of people who deliver, fund, and use healthcare.

1. **Embrace value for patients as the overarching goal of healthcare.** Value means meeting the needs of patients as efficiently as possible. It is the only goal that resonates with all stakeholders. Clinicians who do not want to think about efficiency are ceding that responsibility to others; this is likely to lead to adverse consequences for patients and a worse professional environment for providers.

Accepting responsibility for quality and cost is the smart and right thing for providers to do. Embracing this goal means plunging in and making it the top priority with which everything else must be aligned.

2. **Embrace market forces as drivers of a new healthcare marketplace.** Providers are unnerved about unintended consequences and potentially perverse outcomes if patients are regarded as consumers who shop for care that they can afford and that meets their needs. However, the reality is that middle-class families cannot afford the full costs of the status quo: health insurance plans with access to any provider and providers who can charge whatever they believe is needed to cover their costs plus a modest margin.

The inevitable consequences of this tension are already playing out. Individual patients/consumers are picking insurance plans that they can afford at open enrollment or on the exchanges, and many of those plans do not include all providers. Employers and payers are starting to steer patients toward providers that accept bundled prices for the care of chronic and acute conditions. Only a small percentage of patients are changing where they get their care as a result of these forces at this point, but it takes only small shifts in volume to destabilize a provider organization that relies on the old model of care.

The implication is that market forces are arriving as real drivers, and providers should do more than accept this reality. Here again, the alternatives are worse for patients and worse for providers. The organizations that will be most successful will be the ones that embrace market forces and look for opportunities to use them to increase their market share by improving their efficiency and the way they meet patients' needs.

3. **Recognize that competition is the secret sauce for a better healthcare system.** If you accept the idea that market forces are the best option for driving healthcare, plunge into competition on the right things. If you don't accept market forces as the best driver, consider carefully the alternatives and their implications. Every path forward has potentially adverse unintended consequences; competition is the only one that offers the potential for major improvements too. Competition in every other business sector leads to better quality at lower cost, and there is no reason that it cannot and will not do the same thing in healthcare.

That is the good news. The tough news is that competition is stressful. It virtually always demands improvement, and improvement requires change. Change is miserable for good hardworking people who are already overwhelmed by their work. (One of my colleagues likes to say, "All change is bad, including change for the better.") However, inability to change is a losing game plan in a competitive environment, and change for the better can win market share, improve margins, and enhance professional pride.

Forward-looking organizations should recognize the opportunity in competition. If they see that opportunity and respond to it before their competitors do, they will have an advantage in organizing their personnel to thrive in the new marketplace. The goal, of course, is not to separate providers into winners and losers but to drive improvement, and competition does a much better job of driving improvement than setting some floor of minimum performance that is sufficient to avoid penalties.

4. **Embrace empathic, coordinated care as a core component of high-value healthcare.** The hard clinical outcomes such as mortality and complications matter

most, and providers must be reliably excellent in following guidelines and delivering evidence-based medicine, but that is not enough. Providers have to be tuned in to other types of outcomes that matter to patients, including the disutility of care: the anxiety, the confusion, and the uncertainty about what is happening next. Clinicians know that these issues matter. When the clinicians themselves are ill or their friends or family members require care, they do all they can to ensure that these issues are addressed.

Recognizing patient suffering and anticipating, mitigating, and preventing it are acts consistent with the highest professional values of clinicians. Empathy is thus a core element of excellence. One cannot have high-value healthcare that does not address these types of outcomes. Providers are unlikely to be able to hold on to their market share or gain the trust of more patients without making empathic care part of their strategic vision.

5. **Measure the outcomes that matter to patients.** Peace of mind and trust are difficult to measure, but there are reasonable markers available; likelihood to recommend may be the best. Clinicians should get over their concern that patients cannot judge quality as well as can those with clinical training. Likelihood of recommending and other patient experience variables reflect the extent to which patients believe that their needs are being met. If patients do not believe their needs are being met, it is hard to argue that providers have met them.

The measures will never be perfect. The data will never be perfect. The analytic methods will never be perfect. But collectively, providers and the organizations that help them measure these outcomes should use what is available to improve while also working to improve measurement. Perfection should not be the enemy of the good, and collecting more data can help reduce the chances of being misled by the data. Then the data should be used with wisdom and humility.

6. **Organize patients and providers to improve those outcomes and do so efficiently.** The reason to measure performance is to improve it, and that is not likely to happen if clinicians are pushed to work harder as individuals. What can lead to marked improvement is segmenting patients into groups with similar needs and organizing multidisciplinary teams to meet those needs. Those teams are most likely to be effective if patient volume is concentrated on them and if the key team members are consolidated at one site so that they really know one another, learn to trust one another, and send the same messages to patients. If those teams are rewarded for better performance, whether financially or otherwise, they can often create remarkable improvements in both quality and efficiency.

7. **Make the building of social capital as prominent a concern for the organization as financial goals are.** Ultimately, the viability of healthcare organizations in a competitive marketplace—and the joy their personnel get from working in them—depends on their ability to create value for patients. To improve—to do more for patients than they currently can do and to do it more efficiently—organizations have to learn, and then they have to standardize around best practices. The themes of Ronald Burt's framework for social capital—brokerage and closure—matter more than bond ratings. Boards of directors, trustees, CEOs, and other senior leaders should recognize the importance of social capital and approach

the work of building it with the same discipline they currently apply to financial capital.

8. **Identify the teams that are the real units of healthcare delivery and use social network science to enhance their effectiveness.** Almost every patient with conditions of any complexity has a team of clinicians today, but those clinicians often do not know that they are part of a team or function like a pickup team of players who are meeting for the first time. Social network science can be used to help teams function better, resulting in better and more efficient care, greater professional pride, and lower personnel turnover.

9. **Use financial incentives for financial issues.** Idealistic and optimistic though I may be, I know that money matters to almost everyone. I am completely comfortable with the use of financial incentives for financial issues, including rewarding hard work and the thoughtful work required to make care more efficient.

10. **Use nonfinancial incentives for nonfinancial issues, including driving the organization's epidemic of empathy.** Improvement of quality, including empathic care, should not be driven by purely financial considerations. No clinician should ever pause to wonder whether he or she should be empathic. Instead, being an empathic clinician should be a social norm. Clinicians and other personnel should work hard as individuals and effectively as teams to reduce patients' suffering because it brings them pride and because if they didn't, they would be ashamed. These intrinsic motivations can produce improvements in quality that financial incentives never will.

The insights of social network science can speed the spread of the norm of empathic care. The most influential clinicians—those who can initiate the process—can be identified just by asking around. A critical mass of empathic clinicians can send the message to everyone else that this is the way we deliver care. Personnel who are isolated can be brought closer to the group so that the norms have a greater impact on them. Peer pressure and transparency can be used to help personnel be at their best not just for special patients but for all patients.

The delivery of healthcare offers an endless series of opportunities for provider personnel to rise to the occasion, meet their patients' needs, and reduce their suffering. Organizations that can help their personnel do that will be rewarded both with business success and with the pride that can result from an epidemic of empathy.

Notes

Introduction

1. Nicholas A. Christakis and James H. Fowler, "The Spread of Obesity in a Large Social Network over 32 Years," *New England Journal of Medicine* 357, July 26, 2007: 370–379. DOI: 10.1056/NEJMsa066082.
2. Nicholas A. Christakis and James H. Fowler, "The Collective Dynamics of Smoking in a Large Social Network," *New England Journal of Medicine* 358, May 22, 2008: 2249–2258. DOI: 10.1056/NEJMsa0706154.
3. *Empathy: The Human Connection to Patient Care.* https://www.youtube.com/watch?v=cDDWvj_q-o8.
4. Thomas H. Lee, "The Word That Shall Not Be Spoken," *New England Journal of Medicine* 369, November 7, 2013:1777–1779. DOI: 10.1056/NEJMp1309660.
5. Gina Kolata, "Doctors Strive to Do Less Harm Through Inattentive Care," *New York Times,* February 18, 2015. Accessed August 7, 2015, http://www.nytimes.com/2015/02/18/health/doctors-strive-to-do-less-harm-by-inattentive-care.html?_r=0.

Chapter 1

1. Beth A. Lown, Julie Rosen, and John Martilla, "An Agenda for Improving Compassionate Care: A Survey Shows About Half of Patients Say Such Care Is Missing," *Health Affairs* 30, September 2011: 1772–1778. DOI: 10.1377/hlthaff.2011.0539.
2. A. McGehee Harvey, *Adventures in Medical Research: A Century of Discovery at Johns Hopkins* (Baltimore: Johns Hopkins Press, 1974): 158.
3. William Osler, "The Lumleian Lectures: On Angina Pectoris," *Lancet* 175, April 9, 1910: 973–977. DOI: 10.1016/S0140-6736(01)14114-0.
4. Tinsley R. Harrison, Paul B. Beeson, William H. Resnik, et al., *Principles of Internal Medicine* (New York: Blakiston, 1950): 1342.

5. Thomas H. Lee, "Turning Doctors into Leaders," *Harvard Business Review*, April 2010: 50–58. Accessed August 7, 2015, https://hbr.org/product/turning -doctors-into-leaders/R1004B-PDF-ENG.

6. Gail Gazelle, Jane M. Liebschutz, and Helen Riess, "Physician Burnout: Coaching a Way Out," *Journal of General Internal Medicine* 30, April 2015: 508–513. DOI: 10.1007/s11606-014-3144-y.

7. Christina Maslach and Michael P. Leiter, *The Truth About Burnout: How Organizations Cause Personal Stress and What to Do About It* (San Francisco: Jossey-Bass, 1997): 186.

8. Emily D. Dolan, David Mohr, Michelle Lempa, et al., "Using a Single Item to Measure Burnout in Primary Care Staff: A Psychometric Evaluation," *Journal of General Internal Medicine* 30, April 2015: 582–587. DOI: 10.1007/s11606- 014-3112-6.

9. Thomas H. Lee and Toby Cosgrove, "Engaging Doctors in the Healthcare Revolution," *Harvard Business Review* 92, June 2014:104–111. Accessed August 7, 2015, https://hbr.org/2014/06/engaging-doctors-in-the-health -care-revolution.

Chapter 2

1. Centers for Medicare and Medicaid, *National Health Expenditures 2013 Highlights*. Accessed August 7, 2015, https://www.cms.gov/ Research-Statistics-Data-and-Systems/Statistics-Trends-and-Reports/ NationalHealthExpendData/downloads/highlights.pdf.

2. Amanda Noss, "Household Income: 2013," *American Community Survey Briefs*, Washington , DC: U.S. Census Bureau, September 2014. Accessed August 7, 2015, https://www.census.gov/content/dam/Census/library/ publications/2014/acs/acsbr13-02.pdf.

3. Michael E. Porter and Thomas H. Lee, "Why Strategy Matters Now," *New England Journal of Medicine* 372, 2015:1681–1684. DOI: 10.1056/ NEJMp1502419.

4. Linda T. Kohn, Janet M. Corrigan, and Molla S. Donaldson (Editors), *To Err Is Human: Building a Safer Health System* (Washington, DC: National Academies Press, 2000). Accessed August 7, 2015, http://www.nap.edu/ openbook.php?record_id=9728.

5. Committee on Quality of Health Care in America, *Crossing the Quality Chasm: A New Health System for the 21st Century* (Washington, DC: National Academies Press, 2001). Accessed August 7, 2015, http://www.nap.edu/ openbook.php?isbn=0309072808.

6. Christine K. Cassel, Patrick H. Conway, Suzanne F. Delbanco, Ashish K. Jha, Robert S. Saunders, and Thomas H. Lee, "Getting More Performance from Performance Measurement," *New England Journal of Medicine* 371, December 4, 2014: 2145–2147. DOI: 10.1056/NEJMp1408345.

7. Michael E. Porter, "What Is Value in Healthcare?" *New England Journal of Medicine* 363, December 23, 2010:2477–2481. DOI: 10.1056/NEJMp1011024.

Chapter 3

1. Richard A. Friedman, "Understanding Empathy: Can You Feel My Pain?" *New York Times*, April 27, 2007. Accessed August 7, 2015, http://www.nytimes.com/2007/04/24/health/24beha.html.

2. Helen Riess, "Empathy in Medicine—a Neurobiological Perspective," *JAMA* 304, October 13, 2010:1604–1605. DOI: 10.1001/jama.2010.1455.

3. Mohammadreza Hojat, *Empathy in Patient Care: Antecedents, Development, Measurement, and Outcomes* (New York: Springer, 2007): 80.

4. Eric B. Larson and Xian Xin Yao, "Clinical Empathy as Emotional Labor in the Patient-Physician Relationship," *JAMA* 293, March 2, 2005:1106–1011. DOI: 10.1001/jama.293.9.1100.

5. Anthony L. Suchman, Kathryn Markakis, Howard B. Beckman, and Richard M. Frankel, "A Model of Empathic Communication in the Medical Interview," *JAMA* 277, February 26, 1997: 678–682. DOI:10.1001/jama.1997.03540320082047.

6. Kathryn I. Pollak, Robert M. Arnold, Amy S. Jeffrey, et al., "Oncologist Communication About Emotions During Visits with Patients with Advanced Cancer," *Journal of Clinical Oncology* 25, December 20, 2007: 6748–6752. DOI: 10.1200/JCO.2007.12.4180.

7. Laura J. McVey, Donald E. Davis, and Harvey Jay Cohen, "The 'Aging Game'—an Approach to Education in Geriatrics," *JAMA* 262, September 15, 1989: 1507–1509. Accessed August 7, 2015. DOI:10.1001/jama.1989.03430110097036.

8. Helen Riess, John M. Kelly, and Robert W. Bailey, "Empathy Training for Resident Physicians: A Randomized Controlled Trial of a Neuroscience-Informed Curriculum," *Journal of General Internal Medicine* 27, October 2012: 1280–1286. Accessed August 7, 2015. DOI: 10.1007/s11606-012-2063-z.

9. Stewart W. Mercer, Margaret Maxwell, David Heaney, et al., "The Consultation and Relational Empathy (CARE) Measure: Development and Preliminary Validation and Reliability of an Empathy-Based Consultation Process Measure," *Family Practice* 21, December 2004: 699–705. DOI: 10.1093/fampra/cmh621.

10. Robert Axelrod, *The Evolution of Cooperation* (New York: Basic Books, 1984).

11. Thomas H. Lee, "The Word That Shall Not Be Spoken," *New England Journal of Medicine* 369, 2013:1777–1779. DOI: 10.1056/NEJMp1309660.

12. *AMA Manual of Style: A Guide for Authors and Editors* (New York: Oxford University Press, 2007): 416–417.

13. Lisa M. Bellini and Judy A. Shea, "Mood Change and Empathy Decline Persist During Three Years of Internal Medicine Training," *Academic Medicine* 80, February 2005:164–167.

14. Sharyn J. Potter and John B. McKinlay, "From a Relationship to Encounter: An Examination of Longitudinal and Lateral Dimensions in the Doctor–Patient Relationship," *Social Science & Medicine* 61, July 2005: 465–479. DOI: 10.1016/j.socscimed.2004.11.067.

15. Sunil Dasan, Poonam Gohil, Victoria Cornelius, et al., "Prevalence, Causes and Consequences of Compassion Satisfaction and Compassion Fatigue in Emergency Care: A Mixed-Methods Study of UK NHS Consultants," *Emergency Medicine Journal* 32, August 2015: 588–594. DOI: 10.1136/emermed-2014-203671.

Chapter 4

1. Howard H. Hiatt, Benjamin A. Barnes, Troyen A. Brennan, et al., "A Study of Medical Injury and Medical Malpractice," *New England Journal of Medicine* 321, 1989: 480-484. DOI: 10.1056/NEJM198908173210725.

2. Michael E. Porter, "What Is Value in Healthcare?" *New England Journal of Medicine* 363, December 23, 2010:2477–2481. DOI: 10.1056/NEJMp1011024.

3. Douglas Stone and Sheila Heen, *Thanks for the Feedback: The Science and Art of Receiving Feedback Well* (New York: Viking Press, 2014).

4. Joshua J. Fenton, Anthony F. Jerant, Klea D. Bertakis, and Peter Franks, "The Cost of Satisfaction: A National Study of Patient Satisfaction, Health Care Utilization, Expenditures, and Mortality," *Archives of Internal Medicine* 172, March 12, 2012: 405–411. DOI: 10.1001/archinternmed.2011.1662.

5. Ashish K. Jha, E. John Orav, Jie Zheng, and Arnold M. Epstein, "Patients' Perception of Hospital Care in the United States," *New England Journal of Medicine* 359, October 30, 2008:1921–1931. DOI: 10.1056/NEJMsa0804116.

6. Greg D. Sacks, Elise H. Lawson, Aaron J. Dawes, Marcia M. Russell, Melinda Maggard-Gibbons, David S. Zingmond, and Clifford Y. Ko, "Patient Satisfaction Survey and Surgical Quality," *JAMA Surgery*. Published online June 24, 2015. DOI:10.1001/jamasurg.2014.1108.

7. Matthew P. Manary, William Boulding, Richard Staelin, and Seth W. Glickman, "The Patient Experience and Health Outcomes," *New England Journal of Medicine* 368, January 17, 2013:201–203. DOI: 10.1056/NEJMp1211775.

8. Tayler M. Schwartz, Miao Tai, Kavita M. Babu, and Roland C. Merchant, "Lack of Association Between Press Ganey Emergency Department Patient Satisfaction Scores and Emergency Department Administration of Analgesic Medications," *Annals of Emergency Medicine* 64, May 2014: 469–481. DOI: 0.1016/j.annemergmed.2014.02.010.

9. C. Komal Jaipaul and Gary E. Rosenthal, "Do Hospitals with Lower Mortality Have Higher Patient Satisfaction? A Regional Analysis of Patients with Medical Diagnoses," *American Journal of Medical Quality* 18, March/April 2003: 59–65. DOI: 10.1177/106286060301800203.

10. Seth W. Glickman, William Boulding, Matthew Manary, Richard Staelin, Matthew T. Roe, Robert J. Wolosin, E. Magnus Ohman, et al., "Patient Satisfaction and Its Relationship with Clinical Quality and Inpatient Mortality in Acute Myocardial Infarction," *Cardiovascular Quality and Outcomes* 3, March 2010: 188–195. DOI: 10.1161/CIRCOUTCOMES.109.900597.

11. Klea D. Bertakis and Rahman Azari, "Patient-Centered Care Is Associated with Decreased Health Care Utilization," *Journal of the American Board of Family Medicine* 24, May–June 2011: 229–239. DOI: 10.3122/jabfm.2011.03.100170.

12. Jane C. Weeks, Paul J. Catalano, Angel Cronin, Matthew D. Finkelman, Jennifer W. Mack, Nancy L. Keating, and Deborah Schrag, "Patients' Expectations About Effects of Chemotherapy for Advanced Cancer," *New England Journal of Medicine* 367:1616–1625. DOI: 10.1056/NEJMoa120441.

13. Deirdre E. Mylod and Thomas H. Lee, "A Framework for Reducing Suffering in Healthcare," *Harvard Business Review*, November 14, 2013. Accessed August 7, 2015, https://hbr.org/2013/11/a-framework-for-reducing-suffering-in-health-care.

Chapter 5

1. Ronald S. Burt, *Brokerage and Closure* (Oxford: Oxford University Press, 2005): 15.

2. Melissa D. Phipps and John D. Phipps, "Code Comfort—A Code Blue Alternative for Patients with DNRs," *Harvard Business Review*, December 9, 2014. Accessed August 7, 2015, https://hbr.org/2014/12/code-comfort-a-code-blue-alternative-for-patients-with-dnrs.

3. Anna M. Roth and Thomas H. Lee, "Healthcare Needs Less Innovation and More Imitation," *Harvard Business Review*, November 19, 2014. Accessed August 7, 2015, https://hbr.org/2014/11/health-care-needs-less-innovation-and-more-imitation.

4. Ronald S. Burt, *Brokerage and Closure* (Oxford: Oxford University Press, 2005): 93.

5. Nicholas A. Christakis and James H. Fowler, *Connected: The Surprising Power of Our Social Networks and How They Shape Our Lives* (New York: Little, Brown and Company, 2009).

6. Susan Dominus, "What Happened to the Girls in Le Roy," *New York Times Magazine*, March 7, 2012. Accessed August 7, 2015, http://www.nytimes.com/2012/03/11/magazine/teenage-girls-twitching-le-roy.html.

7. Channel 4, *The Town That Caught Tourette's*. Accessed August 7, 2015, https://www.youtube.com/watch?v=T4-v5FriLrk.

8. Nicholas A. Christakis and James H. Fowler, "The Spread of Obesity in a Large Social Network over 32 Years," *New England Journal of Medicine* 357, July 26, 2007: 370–379. DOI: 10.1056/NEJMsa066082.

9. Nicholas A. Christakis and James H. Fowler, "Social Contagion Theory: Examining Dynamic Social Networks and Human Behavior," *Statistics in Medicine* 32, February 20, 2013: 581–590. DOI: 10.1002/sim.5408.

10. Nicholas A. Christakis, James H. Fowler, and Rose McDermott, "Breaking Up Is Hard to Do, Unless Everyone Else Is Doing It Too: Social Network Effects on Divorce in a Longitudinal Sample," *Social Forces* 92, December 2013: 491–519. DOI: 10.2139/ssrn.1490708.

11. David A. Kim, Alison R. Hwong, Derek Stafford, D. Alex Hughes, A. James O'Malley, James H. Fowler, and Nicholas A. Christakis, "Social Network Targeting to Maximise Population Behaviour Change: A Cluster Randomised Controlled Trial," *Lancet* 386, July 11, 2015:145–153. DOI: 10.1016/S0140-6736(15)60095-2.

12. James H. Fowler and Nicholas A. Christakis, "Dynamic Spread of Happiness in a Large Social Network: Longitudinal Analysis over 20 Years in the Framingham Heart Study," *British Medical Journal* 337, December 8, 2008:123–138. DOI: 10.1136/bmj.a2338.

13. John T. Cacioppo, James H. Fowler, and Nicholas A. Christakis, "Alone in the Crowd: The Structure and Spread of Loneliness in a Large Social Network," *Journal of Personality and Social Psychology* 97, December 2009: 977-991. DOI: 10.1037/a0016076.

14. Marina Keegan, "The Opposite of Loneliness," *Yale Daily News*, May 27, 2012. Accessed August 7, 2015, http://yaledailynews.com/crosscampus/2012/05/27/keegan-the-opposite-of-loneliness/.

Chapter 6

1. Thomas H. Lee and Toby Cosgrove, "Engaging Doctors in the Healthcare Revolution," *Harvard Business Review* 92, June 2014:104–111. Accessed August 7, 2015, https://hbr.org/2014/06/engaging-doctors-in-the-health -care-revolution; Nikola Biller-Andorno and Thomas H. Lee, "Ethical Physician Incentives—from Carrots and Sticks to Shared Purpose," *New England Journal of Medicine* 368, March 13, 2013: 980–982. DOI: 10.1056/ NEJMp1300373.

2. Eric Goralnick, Ron M. Walls, and Joshua M. Kosowsky, "How We Revolutionized Our Emergency Department," *Harvard Business Re*view, September 26, 2013. Accessed August 7, 2015, https://hbr.org/2013/09/ how-we-revolutionized-our-emergency-department/.

3. Thomas H. Lee, Albert Bothe, and Glenn D. Steele, "How Geisinger Structures Its Physicians' Compensation to Support Improvements in

Quality, Efficiency, and Volume," *Health Affairs* 31, September 2012: 2068–2073. DOI: 10.1377/hlthaff.2011.0940.

4. Rosemary Thackeray, Benjamin Crookston, and Joshua West, "Correlates of Health-Related Social Media Use Among Adults," *Journal of Medical Internet Research* 15, January 2013: e21. DOI: 10.2196/jmir.2297.

5. David. A. Hanauer, Kai Zheng, Dianne C. Singer, Achamyeleh Gebremariam, and Matthew M. Davis, "Public Awareness, Perception, and Use of Online Physician Rating Sites," *JAMA* 311, February 19, 2014: 734–735. DOI: 10.1001/jama.2013.283194.

6. Eric Anderson and Duncan Simester, "Reviews Without a Purchase: Low Ratings, Loyal Customers, and Deception," *Journal of Marketing Research* 51, June 2014: 249–269. DOI: http://dx.doi.org/10.1509/jmr.13.0209.

Index

About the Author

THOMAS H. LEE, MD, is chief medical officer of Press Ganey Associates, Inc. He is an internist and cardiologist, and practices primary care at Brigham and Women's Hospital in Boston. Before assuming his role at Press Ganey, he was network president for Partners Healthcare System, the integrated delivery system founded by Brigham and Women's Hospital and Massachusetts General Hospital. He is a graduate of Harvard College, Cornell University Medical College, and Harvard School of Public Health. Dr. Lee is also a professor of medicine (part time) at Harvard Medical School and a professor of health policy and management at Harvard School of Public Health.

Dr. Lee is a member of the board of directors of Geisinger Health System, the board of overseers of Weill Cornell Medical College, Special Medical Advisory Committee (SMAC) of the

Veterans Administration, the board of directors of Health Leads, and the Panel of Health Advisors of the Congressional Budget Office.

He also serves on the editorial board of the *New England Journal of Medicine*. He is the author, with James J. Mongan, MD, of *Chaos and Organization in Health Care* (MIT Press, 2009) and the author of *Eugene Braunwald and the Rise of Modern Medicine* (Harvard University Press, 2013).